• *Saving* •

STUART
F L O R I D A

Rebuilding America's Happiest Seaside Town

BLAKE FONTENAY

THE
History
PRESS

Published by The History Press
Charleston, SC
www.historypress.com

Front cover images by Crystal Vander Weit.

First published 2025

Manufactured in the United States

ISBN 9781467155816

Library of Congress Control Number: 2024944895

Notice: The information in this book is true and complete to the best of our knowledge. It is offered without guarantee on the part of the author or The History Press. The author and The History Press disclaim all liability in connection with the use of this book.

This book is dedicated to Richard Chambers,
one of many great teachers I've had during my lifetime.
Aside from helping me avoid coming completely unglued during high school,
he instilled in me a love of history that endures to this day.

CONTENTS

CONTENTS

ACKNOWLEDGEMENTS

One of the advantages of writing about history from the not-too-distant past is there are still people around who can provide first-person accounts of what transpired. Although much of my research for this book involved reading old newspaper clippings, there are also numerous first-person interviews with people who lived and worked in Stuart during the 1980s and 1990s. All of them were so generous with their time. Even a few whose names don't appear in the book were helpful in providing details about life in Stuart during that time.

I would like to offer special thanks to Julie Preast, who, in addition to sharing her recollections as a downtown business owner, also suggested names of others she thought could be helpful in my research. Joan Jefferson's name pops up a lot in this book—and for good reason. After my initial interview with her, I spent weeks peppering her with follow-up questions, asking her to recall specifics from events that happened more than four decades ago. Joan also loaned me a box full of files she kept on various topics from that period. Although I had no idea such a box existed when I began this project, I'm now having trouble imagining how I could have done this without Joan's files.

Any mistakes made in this book are the result of my errors, not those I interviewed.

Thanks so much to the staff at the Martin County Library System and Mia Tignor, archivist at Indian River State College, for helping me with the photos. Mia, in particular, is no doubt sick of seeing my number in her caller

ID. Sandra Thurlow, a local author who has probably forgotten more about Stuart history than I'll ever know, was extremely generous in sharing photos she has collected through the years.

Thanks to my sister, Gretchen, who is also a writer, for keeping me motivated by asking, "How's the book going?" whenever we talked over the last few months. Thanks to my wife, Lynn, who tolerates all my extra weirdness when I'm in book-writing mode.

Thanks to my boss, Adam, for giving me a flexible work schedule that made this project possible. Thanks to my Hell Gate Sea Dragons dragon boat coaches and teammates, especially Bob and Diane, for understanding why I needed to skip Saturday practices when my deadline was approaching.

Going back a little further in time, thank you to my former co-workers at the Tennessee State Library and Archives, who taught me much about historical research through osmosis. Thanks to former Stuart city commissioner Troy McDonald, who got me started on this crazy idea in the first place by sharing what he knew about downtown Stuart's transformation during the 1980s and 1990s.

And thanks, of course, to Joe Gartrell and the staff of The History Press. Joe has been a patient editor and managed to work with me despite my almost complete computer illiteracy. I'm sure there are others I'm forgetting, but thanks to all my supportive friends and neighbors. I hope you enjoy reading this book as much as I enjoyed writing it!

A STORY OF ABUNDANT RESILIENCE

Lady Abundance is a nice symbol for the neighborhood where she stands. The beautiful statue is in Haney Circle, a scenic roundabout on Osceola Street, anchoring one end of the historic shopping district in downtown Stuart, Florida.

Like her more famous counterpart, the Statue of Liberty, Lady Abundance was a gift to America from the French. Lady Abundance was originally brought to the United States for display at the 1939 World's Fair in New York, but years later, the Women's Club of Stuart bought the statue and brought her to the little coastal town about one hundred miles north of Miami.

The first attempt to display her at Haney Circle resulted in scandal. Lady Abundance depicts a woman who is possibly pregnant and definitely carrying a couple of jugs of wine. Since the circle was named for Cynthia Haney, a childless prohibitionist, the statue's placement there wasn't a great fit on either of those counts.

Also, the thinking in the 1950s was that she was a bit too…abundant for local tastes. "With its tight-fitting dress and healthy curves, the statue has raised questions of propriety through the years," the *Stuart News* noted in a July 5, 1990 article.

When Lady Abundance was on public display, there were some in the community who took matters into their own hands to address her apparent lack of modesty. "Everyone used to go in and dress it," said Dale Hudson, president of First National Bank and Trust Co. of the Treasure Coast, in that 1990 *News* article. "She was considered indecent."

Lady Abundance at Haney Circle, September 10, 1993. *Sandra Thurlow photo collection.*

So the statuesque statue was relocated to a site near the local courthouse, where, according to the *Palm Beach Post*, "she suffered rude remarks from jail inmates."

She was later moved to Memorial Park for a while before ending up in a warehouse, where she lay covered with dirt for decades. Gone, but not forgotten. By 1990, a group of downtown merchants were lobbying to bring her out of storage and return her to her old haunt in Haney Circle.

"My partner is in love with her," Bob Flagg, co-owner of Huston's Office Supply, said that year.

Joan Jefferson, a Stuart city commissioner and downtown advocate, said what the statue represented was too important to suppress. "Lady Bountiful [*sic*] has been pregnant for 30 years or more; the controversy should have ended by now," Jefferson said. "We [the city] are pregnant with promise and she is a symbol of that pregnancy."

In 1991, she was liberated from her impromptu grave, cleaned up and returned to her perch in Haney Circle.

Downtown Stuart is a lot like that statue in some ways. It has a rich history, but there was also a time when the neighborhood seemed to be on its way out. Lady Abundance returned to Haney Circle while downtown Stuart was in the middle of a transformation.

The 1980s were interesting times in South Florida. On the hit TV show *Miami Vice*, detectives Crockett and Tubbs chased bad guys (and gals) through the region's seamy underworld, while at the same time showcasing for a national audience how cool modern-day Miami was. Less than two hours' drive away, coolness was in short supply in the riverfront town of Stuart.

Malls and strip shopping centers were taking the place of traditional shopping districts all over the country, with Stuart being no exception. Businesses had largely abandoned the downtown area's historic buildings, leaving the streets deserted and dark. Treasure Coast Square, a new mall a few miles north of town, was about to make the challenges of running a small business in the center city even greater.

A 1987 report on the city's future economic prospects by a Tallahassee consulting firm sounded almost like an obituary. "If present trends continue, all remnants of a downtown commercial and service center could be lost," read the report by Clark, Roumelis & Associates.

The St. Lucie River, which should have been one of the town's greatest assets, was more of a liability fouled with pollution from many sources, including the city's own sewer system. The southernmost leg of Interstate 95 hadn't been completed yet, meaning US 1, the town's main thoroughfare, was clogged with traffic that had no intention of stopping in this dirty backwater.

The Roosevelt Bridge spanning the river badly needed replacement, but how that was done could make or break the fragile local economy. Downtown Stuart was so down and out that Martin County government was thinking of relocating its courthouse to a different spot.

Fortunately, there were people committed to seeing Stuart reborn. One was Joan Jefferson, a secretary in her husband's architectural firm. The couple had moved north because they didn't like the way the Miami area was growing and changing. They and another couple eventually moved into the Post Office Arcade building, one of the historic structures in danger of falling into decay. They were among the first local urban pioneers.

In time, Joan Jefferson would become Stuart's mayor, overseeing a rebirth that has made Stuart a regular on national "best small town" lists. She didn't make the change happen all by herself, but she was a key player in rallying residents to change the town's trajectory. From the mid-1980s to the mid-1990s, Stuart residents made a series of good decisions (including following the advice of renowned urban planner Andrés Duany, father of Seaside) and pushed back against naysayers, unscrupulous developers and clueless state bureaucrats.

Old courthouse annex being razed. *Sandra Thurlow photo collection.*

It wasn't easy. In the beginning, some saw the city's downtown as a lost cause. There were disagreements about what, if anything, could be done to bring downtown back to life. Yet Stuart's supporters persevered, thanks to a combination of teamwork, good ideas and no small measure of good fortune.

In 2015, *Smithsonian Magazine* listed Stuart in its "Best Small Towns to Visit" guide. In 2016, *Coastal Living* magazine dubbed Stuart the "Happiest Seaside Town in America." SmartAsset listed Stuart as one of "10 Best Places to Retire in Florida" in 2018. Stuart won the "Great Places in Florida Award," sponsored by the American Planning Associations' Florida chapter, in 2020. Stuart was first in *USA TODAY*'s ranking of "Best Coastal Small Towns" in 2024.

Downtown Stuart, like Lady Abundance, has made a comeback. This is its story.

Chapter 1

THE JEFFERSONS WERE MOVIN' ON UP

I t isn't possible to tell the story about what happened to downtown Stuart in the late 1980s and early 1990s without talking about Joan and Peter Jefferson.

When entering downtown Stuart from the north today, the first major intersection motorists reach after crossing the Roosevelt Bridge on US 1 is Joan Jefferson Way. That's a fitting metaphor. Jeffrey Krauskopf, who served on the Stuart City Commission with Joan Jefferson during the pivotal years of downtown's revitalization, said this about his former colleague: "She was not a key figure. She was *the* key figure."

The Jeffersons were involved, in one way or another, in just about every major development that happened downtown during that transformational era. A *Palm Beach Post* headline once described the Jeffersons as "Stuart's first family," a title that held up before, during and after Joan Jefferson's tenure as mayor.

The Jeffersons were among the city's most influential power couples at that time, with their words and actions taking on almost folk hero status. One newspaper article described Peter Jefferson as a "Santa Claus look alike." Peter didn't exactly shy away from such comparisons. He attended Santa Claus University to learn the proper etiquette for the role. He served as Santa in the Stuart Christmas Parade. He even took a turn playing Santa at Macy's Department Store in New York City.

"He was intelligent, perceptive, eternally curious and a little whacky— all characteristics that make a good Santa," Joan Jefferson said of her late husband.

As for Joan, the *Stuart News* described her in one article as "tall, auburn haired with green eyes and talks in a low-key sexy voice."

Neither of the Jeffersons was native to Stuart, though. Peter Jefferson moved to Florida from Wheeling, West Virginia, in 1954. He attended Washington & Jefferson University and then spent about three and a half years studying architecture at the University of Michigan. He became interested in architecture after seeing an exhibition by the renowned Frank Lloyd Wright at the university. "[Wright's] work also convinced me that formal education was not the best way to go," Peter told a reporter years later.

Peter had worked as a brick tender, a carpenter's helper, an assistant cement finisher and a draftsman, so he was well acquainted with other aspects of construction beyond just design. He got his Florida architectural license in 1959. Later, he had a fellowship with the American Institute of Architects.

Peter expressed a dislike for cold and sterile design elements. He wasn't a fan of chrome, vinyl or Formica. Through the years, he developed an interest in designing "in harmony with the climate." "His works relate directly to his own nature: open, sensitive, complex, dignified, strongly responsive to the environment, original," Peter wrote in a rough draft of his bio.

He met Joan, who had grown up in Pittsfield, Massachusetts, at a social mixer in Coconut Grove, a Miami suburb where both were living. The two discovered they had a lot in common. Although Joan had attended convent school from ages thirteen to sixteen, where she learned "I did not like scrubbing floors with a toothbrush," she was much a free spirit.

Joan liked to cook "for therapy" but also had other interests that were far more adventurous. She tried skydiving in Fort Lauderdale and motorcycle racing in California. At one point in her career, she sold airplanes.

Joan and Peter shared a love of travel, preferring back roads over interstates. They loved touring the country in an RV they named Carrot.

Following their courtship, the couple got married in Prague, Czechoslovakia. They returned to Coconut Grove after the wedding but eventually became disillusioned with their surroundings. The Miami area was growing fast, with high-rise housing developments sprouting up everywhere. The couple called these "big uglies." And one day, they'd had enough of looking at them.

"A mother should be able to read the expression on a child's face out the back door," Joan said in explaining why the Miami area no longer seemed well suited to the couple's needs.

Courthouse annex during its previous life as an A&P grocery store. *Sandra Thurlow photo collection.*

In a February 17, 1974 *New York Times* article, Joan described Miami as "a diseased community." "Even the sun is being blotted out by smog," she complained.

The Jeffersons' first visit to Stuart didn't happen without a few hitches, though. They arrived in the late 1960s, wearing beads and long hair. That may have been acceptable in many hippie enclaves during that period, but Stuart was a bit more conservative and buttoned down.

On a house-hunting excursion, they asked a local pharmacist about a home that caught their interest. The pharmacist reportedly told them the owner "wouldn't rent it to you, she wouldn't sell it to you, and three years ago, you wouldn't have been allowed in here." It wasn't the warmest of welcomes, but the Jeffersons felt drawn to Stuart anyway.

While the Jeffersons told reporters Coconut Grove was infected with a "physic sickness," Joan gushed about Stuart as a place where "otters and alligators are our neighbors."

They purchased a little house at 35 East Ocean Boulevard to use as an office and temporary residence. Their first night in town, they parked their car on the street and went to bed. The next morning, they discovered their car was gone. They called the police to report the car as stolen but learned that was not the case. The police had towed and impounded the car.

When they went to the station to retrieve the vehicle, the police chief grilled them about a set of bones that had been found in the trunk. At some point during their earlier travels, the Jeffersons had come across a manatee skeleton that Peter was hoping to turn into a mobile. Eventually, the couple convinced the police the bones were not leftovers from some illegal activity and got their car back. The encounter didn't sour them on Stuart.

If the locals thought the Jeffersons were strange, the feeling was mutual. Joan likened the town, with its motley cast of characters, to the bar from the original *Star Wars* movie. But in its strangeness, the Jeffersons also discovered charm.

One of the county commissioners rode to meetings on horseback. The sheriff ran the local bolita game. And then there was the restaurant on US 1 where patrons could feed the mascot, Ruby the Pig. That was, until Ruby bit a child and ended up on the menu herself.

"We thought we were in heaven," Joan said of the couple's overall impression of the town. "Peter wanted to prevent it from becoming hell."

The Jeffersons became outspoken advocates for responsible planning and growth. They were particularly concerned about how the changing climate could impact development on Florida's barrier islands, including Stuart's portion of Hutchinson Island.

Joan was the office manager at Peter's architectural office, handling the business side of the operation. "Peter had no interest in money. I did," Joan quipped decades later. The firm took on dozens of projects during its early years, with a philosophy of designing "in harmony with the climate."

The Jeffersons refurbished a collection of houses, built from 1895 to 1925, on Berry Road in Palm City and leased them out as commercial spaces in what was known as Common Place. Jefferson's firm designed Angler's Cove and Hutchinson House. It was involved in a restoration project at the Gilbert's Bar House of Refuge, which is thought to be the oldest building in Martin County.

The firm's roster of early clients included Ralph Evinrude, the chief executive officer of the famous boat motor company and husband of Frances Langford, an actress once known as "America's sweetheart." Peter Jefferson designed a home for Evinrude, as well as one farther up the coast for *USA TODAY* founder Al Neuharth in Cocoa Beach.

The Jeffersons eventually settled into a house Peter designed along the south fork of the St. Lucie River, surrounded on three sides by water. The house, featured in *Home & Garden* magazine, was filled with quirky Jeffersonian touches, like an old-fashioned bathtub on the veranda and stuffed animals scattered throughout. There was a dock where Peter kept a rowboat moored. The couple's three children lived in separate quarters on the property.

Peter claimed to have fifty-seven chairs between the couple's home in Stuart and a summer home in North Carolina. "Fifty-seven chairs for two sets of buns, this makes no sense to me," Joan once told a reporter with a sly grin on her face.

By the late 1970s and early 1980s, the Jeffersons were on their way to becoming embedded among the community's movers and shakers. The couple's exploits frequently made the newspapers, even the ones that were on the lighthearted side. For example, the *Miami Herald* reported on the time Joan picketed outside her husband's office in the rain. The sign she carried explained the situation: "Peter Jefferson Is Unfair to His Sweet Charming Wife Who Works Long Arduous Hours with No Pay." The article, which described Joan as "the statuesque redhead, who may rank as the most attractive picket since the Las Vegas showgirl walkout," concluded with Peter agreeing to buy a lamp for Joan's office, which apparently ended the impromptu strike.

A 1976 feature story on the couple in *Indian River Life* magazine noted Peter and Joan were so close "you cannot imagine one without the other." Each year, the Jeffersons renewed their wedding vows on their anniversary.

The Jeffersons were playful and fun, but they were also forming some serious ideas about what they wanted their community to look like. In an article that appeared in the *Stuart News* on November 16, 1969, Peter told the Stuart Garden Club population density was "a disease" killing America's cities. "At some point, the whole Earth will be as crowded as Harlem, unless we control births," Peter was quoted as saying.

In the same speech, he envisioned Florida's east coast becoming a "linear city," stretching from Jacksonville to Miami. "Stuart will then become a suburb, a resort or what?" he mused.

To avoid such a fate, Peter said people needed to resist their parasitic tendencies and learn to develop communities that were in harmony with nature. "The only non-suicidal alternative is to plan with nature instead of against it," he said. "We may still be in a period of grace. In that time, let us learn that the proper use of technology is not to conquer the world, but to live in it."

Osceola Furniture Company, Minschke Building. *Sandra Thurlow photo collection.*

Peter lived his philosophy in ways large and small. One of his smaller projects was designing footpaths at the beach to protect native plants from being trampled. One of his larger projects was designing a new county law enforcement complex, with an "extremely experimental" approach to the jail.

According to a 1972 newspaper article about the project, Peter once had a sign in his office with the following Dostoevsky quote: "The degree of civilization in a society can be judged by entering its prisons." His vision for the jail included yellow bars, bright white walls, cable television, piped-in music and even murals for prisoners to enjoy. "It's not the cage, but the atmosphere that determines whether a prisoner is going to be helped by his confinement," Peter said, adding that brighter surroundings could help in the rehabilitation process. "It's a recognition thing—the prisoners are anonymous and by showing them you care with paintings, you're showing them you think of them as individuals," Peter said. "You're giving something to a person in jail and it's something this person can think about."

Roy Baker, the sheriff at the time, seemed somewhat underwhelmed with Peter's vision. "A jail is no place for pretty pictures and murals," he was quoted as saying.

A lot of Peter's ideas were unconventional and outside mainstream thinking, but that served him well as he and Joan became more deeply involved in their adopted community. After their arrival in Stuart, Joan opened the Jefferson Gallery in 1968. In typical Jeffersonian fashion, she created a stir by displaying nude paintings in her art gallery. That might not have been a bigger deal in larger metropolitan areas around the world, but Stuart at the time was still very small and conservative, as the furor over Lady Abundance demonstrated.

Joan also took an interest in some of the major community debates during the late 1960s and early 1970s, such as building height limits (still a political "third rail" in Martin County) and needed infrastructure improvements. She said she got involved in local politics because she wanted Stuart to avoid becoming overrun with development like communities farther south, including her former hometown of Coconut Grove.

She started attending many of the city's various board and commission meetings. But she wasn't content to sit in silence as others plotted out the community's future. "I got pretty mouthy at some of those meetings," Joan said. "Somebody said: 'If you're going to get involved, why don't you get involved?'"

In 1974, Joan made her first bid for elected office, challenging Maggy Hurchalla for a seat on the Martin County Commission. Hurchalla, younger sister to future U.S. attorney general Janet Reno, was in the process of establishing herself as an avid environmentalist and foe of unbridled growth and development. Joan lost that race but didn't lose her interest in politics or government. Five years later, Joan won a seat on the Stuart City Commission, becoming the first woman to hold that position.

Under Stuart's manager-commission form of government, the five commissioners select the mayor from among their ranks. Two years into her tenure as a commissioner, Joan's peers chose her to serve as mayor. Again, Joan was the first woman to hold that position.

As fate had it, she was taking the city's top elected post at a time when a shakeup of some kind was desperately needed.

Chapter 2

A BOWLING ALLEY WITHOUT PINS

Like a lot of cities in Florida, Stuart's early development was linked to the Florida East Coast Railway's expansion. Stuart was incorporated as a city in 1914, two decades after the railroad first reached the community. Trains made travel much easier during a time when cars were still a relatively new technology and roads through the marshland were few.

Stuart was a popular spot for pineapple farming and fishing in its early days. The city, located where the St. Lucie River empties into the Indian River Lagoon and the Atlantic Ocean, still retains the nickname "the Sailfish Capital of the World."

The region's pineapple industry declined for a variety of reasons. As mild as the climate was, it wasn't immune to occasional freezes that could devastate crops. Diseases, like citrus greening, also took a toll. In time, American citrus growers found it difficult to compete with countries farther south, where labor was cheaper. All of this coincided, more or less, with the United States gradually shifting from a rural to an industrialized society.

Heading into the last quarter of the twentieth century, Stuart seemed to be struggling to find its identity in the modern world.

"It was podunk," said Nancy Smith, who began work as a reporter at the *Stuart News* in 1977. "But people also described it as an undiscovered paradise. And they liked it that way."

"Back then, Stuart was pretty much a ghost town," said Jim Dirks, who decided to move to the community after vacationing there in 1977. After working for a few years on a boat and then as a solar panel installer, Dirks decided to get an indoor job after being diagnosed with skin cancer. He opened his shop, Stuart Stained Glass, in 1982.

The businesses that were trying to make it work downtown were a colorful bunch. Dirks described La Petit Café, where corned beef hash, eggs and toast were favored menu items, as "the hub of the wheel."

Stuart Locksmith was a shop known for hosting birthday parties for dogs. Jack Stewart Jewelers was run by an ex-cop who, as legend had it, once stopped a train for speeding and on a separate occasion drove his motorcycle into a hotel pool on Hutchinson Island.

For some people coming to Stuart, the lack of activity was part of the allure. Julie Preast said she moved to the community in the late 1970s for "the same thing that attracts everybody else. I was getting out of Miami. [Stuart] was quiet. It was safe." Preast purchased Pipette, a children's clothing store located downtown next to the city's historic Lyric Theatre, in 1981.

Flagler and Osceola Streets qualified as the main drags downtown, although that was a relative comparison. "Parking was obviously not an issue," Preast said. "It was a small enough town that my clerks pretty much knew everybody by name."

Dirks, the stained-glass store owner, believes he was the first to say that someone could roll a bowling ball down Osceola during those lean years without striking a single person. Whether he coined the expression or not, it was widely used to describe downtown Stuart's lack of activity.

Nationwide, shopping centers and malls were coming into their own during those years, not only as places where people could buy goods and services, but also as spots to gather and socialize.

It's no accident that *Fast Times at Ridgemont High*, a popular movie from the early 1980s, included numerous key scenes from the local mall. At the time, malls were popular teenage hangouts. Stuart was no different in that respect. Ocean East Mall, Martin Square and Regency were among the shopping centers that opened in different locations around the city. The Treasure Coast Mall in nearby Jensen Beach and the Orange Blossom Mall in Fort Pierce started drawing customers away from the city after they opened.

Thomas Weber, former editor of the *Stuart News*, remembers moving to the city in 1966, when "downtown was an active, going place."

But those shopping centers and malls preferred to locate along major roadways, to attract the attention of passing motorists. US 1, the city's main thoroughfare, bypassed the central business district. Downtown Stuart's shops and restaurants were having a tough time competing with the new businesses in outlying neighborhoods and neighboring cities.

Martin County Courthouse, November 11, 1990. *Sandra Thurlow photo collection.*

"Downtown started to look shabbier and shabbier," Weber said. "No one knew what to do about it until the Jeffersons came along."

Dirks said downtown businesses tried various promotions to bring in customers, including turkey giveaways, a "Mother of the Year" competition and a publicity stunt where two men parachuted into Confusion Corner, a fabled intersection near the cluster of shops along Osceola and Flagler. "Anything to draw people to the downtown area," he said.

Stuart's story isn't unique, of course. Lots of cities throughout the country have had trouble protecting their downtown areas from blight. Some were unsuccessful—and the blight spread to other neighborhoods. In the saddest cases, some cities have been reduced to virtual ghost towns.

Stuart's citizens weren't resigned to such a fate. They were about to get an opportunity early in the 1980s to show their love and commitment to their city.

Chapter 3

A REVOLTING START TO DOWNTOWN'S REVIVAL

On December 16, 1773, American colonists expressed their displeasure with British taxation by dumping 342 chests of tea into the Boston Harbor. The protest became known as the Boston Tea Party, a precursor to the American Revolution.

The revitalization of downtown Stuart was a revolution of sorts, too. And it was preceded by another dumping incident, albeit of a much more disgusting kind.

In 1974, Stuart constructed the city's first sewage treatment plant. The city was planning to dispose of its treated sewage by pumping it into a so-called deep injection well, three thousand feet underground. However, the well built by CH2M, a Gainesville firm, didn't work the way it was supposed to. Debris and rubble clogged it up, so the state Department of Environmental Regulation (DER) wouldn't give the city a permit to operate the well.

Instead, the city was dumping its treated wastewater—about 1.3 million gallons per day—into the St. Lucie River. The city needed permission from the state agency for that disposal method, too. And city leaders knew they would need to increase the volume of treated wastewater to keep pace with the town's projected population growth. The city petitioned the DER for permission to dump up to 4 million gallons of treated sewage per day into the river, the amount the city's residents were expected to produce by 2000.

That's when the effluent hit the proverbial fan.

Sewall's Point, a coastal community to Stuart's north, wasn't excited about the prospects of Stuart being able to triple discharges into the river and the adjoining Indian River Lagoon.

"We don't need Stuart's sewage on our shores," Sewall's Point mayor Ed Gluckler was quoted as saying in the May 8, 1980 edition of the *Palm Beach Post*. "Environmental groups and the Martin County Taxpayers Association will oppose this."

In addition to the dumping being an environmental hazard, Gluckler noted the odor from the treatment plant's operations was none too pleasant. "The smell will knock you out some days," he said.

The Sewall's Point mayor wasn't wrong about the uproar in response to Stuart's plans. Environmental groups shared Sewall's Point's concerns about the increased sewage dumping. That was during an era when other coastal cities and industries were coming under increased scrutiny for polluting bodies of water with sewer discharges.

Stuart officials weren't entirely sympathetic to those concerns. In the *Post*'s May 8, 1980 story, Stuart Public Works director Sandy Mitchell suggested the sewage dumping might actually be beneficial to the river. According to tests, Mitchell said, the effluent "has less of some of the bad things than the river water."

Post Office Arcade, September 19, 1992. *Sandra Thurlow photo collection.*

There was also a cost issue to be considered. In a May 14, 1980 *Stuart News* article, Mitchell estimated it would cost the city $2 million more over twenty years to use the well than it would to just keep dumping into the river. "The city doesn't have that kind of money," he complained.

The sewage snafu had serious consequences for the growing city. By March of the following year, the city was forced to impose a moratorium on annexing new territory until the treatment issues could be resolved.

The problem was, there didn't seem to be a lot of great options. With the technology available at the time, the alternatives to using the well included using the effluent as fertilizer for lawns and fields—or allowing it to be gradually absorbed into the ground.

On February 28, 1981, the *Miami Herald* reported that building a spray irrigation system would cost $8.6 million, the "percolation ponds" needed to absorb the sewage into the ground would cost $4.5 million and making improvements to the treatment plant would cost $5 million.

Just fixing the problems with the well would be no small task, either. Consultants told the city the well needed to be about three hundred feet deeper than it was originally dug. Also, the concrete lining along the well's walls needed to be extended from two thousand feet down to three thousand feet in order to work properly. The debris and rubble clogging the passageway needed to be removed, and screens and filters were needed to prevent the problems from recurring.

Enter Joan Jefferson, who by then had been elected to a seat on the Stuart City Commission. Rather than getting into a fight with state regulators, in the fall of 1980, she suggested collaborating with the DER to find the most practical solution. "We should have the best minds in the state to address our problems and show us a way to go and help us fund it," Jefferson was quoted as saying in the October 14, 1980 issue of the *Stuart Evening Times*.

There was a bit of pushback from the state initially. DER officials said they were awaiting instructions from the federal Environmental Protection Agency on how to proceed.

However, by February 1981, the city and DER had reached an agreement that fixing the well was the most practical choice. "It's cheaper to use a hole that's already in the ground than devise a whole new system," DER environmental specialist John Ruddell said in the February 27, 1981 issue of the *Stuart News*.

Although nine other firms bid on the repair work, the city ultimately decided to hire CH2M to fix the problems with the original design.

The city and DER entered into a "consent order" to get the well online. In a letter to state senator John Vogt, Jefferson praised DER for taking a "cooperative rather than adversary [*sic*] approach."

By late 1982, the new well was ready to go into service. The city held a valve-turning ceremony to commemorate the occasion, which was attended by numerous city, county and state officials. After the ceremony, Jefferson and her husband, Peter, treated attendees to a home-cooked meal.

According to an article in the *Palm Beach Post* on December 4, 1982, Peter Jefferson quipped: "The wine we drink today won't surface for 70 years, providing you live inside the city limits."

Stuart finance director Marty Boatright saw some humor in the situation, too. The December 4, 1982 issue of the *Miami Herald* quoted him as saying: "The fish got nothing to eat now."

Thus, one of the stinkiest issues holding back Stuart's progress was resolved.

The city continued to use the revamped well throughout the decade of the 1980s and then added a second well in the early 1990s to increase its wastewater disposal capacity to 13 million gallons per day. In 2012, the city added a reclaimed water irrigation system that could handle another 2.3 million gallons per day.

The wells helped fulfill a basic need all cities must address in one way or another. But Stuart still had numerous other issues that required attention.

As the 1980s progressed, some of them would begin bubbling to the surface.

Chapter 4

WHEN STUART NEEDED HELP, RESIDENTS RESPONDED

To keep downtown Stuart from succumbing to the same types of problems that have killed other downtown areas throughout the United States, a lot of good things had to happen. Community leaders came up with some great ideas for how to address their problems, sometimes on their own and sometimes with the help of outsiders. However, the most important ingredient needed for downtown Stuart's turnaround was the can-do spirit of local business owners and residents.

"I describe it as being in the right place at the right time with the right group of people," said Ann MacMillan, who, with her husband, David, would eventually partner with Joan and Peter Jefferson on one of the riskiest ventures in downtown's revitalization.

Business owners and residents did more than provide moral support for city leaders who needed space to implement some of their big ideas. Many of the townspeople got directly involved, lending either financial support or elbow grease to help make the visionaries' plans come to life.

One of the earliest indicators of how far people were willing to go came in 1983, when Joan Jefferson organized a community service day that she later described as "the happiest and scariest day of my life."

It all started after a Stuart City Commission meeting where there was a discussion about sprucing up the police headquarters. Commissioners realized they didn't have enough money in the city's budget to take care of the necessary work.

Jefferson organized what, in the beginning, she thought would be an event attracting a few dozen people to help out with the renovations. The response was greater than Jefferson had imagined.

"It's going way beyond what we originally thought," Jefferson told the *Stuart News* in the days leading up to the event.

It helped that County Judge Marc Cianca enlisted some "involuntary workers," adults and juveniles whom he had sentenced to do community service work.

"It would be good for the individuals and augment the City's citizen work force for the day," Cianca wrote in an August 2, 1983 letter to Jefferson. "For our juvenile workers I believe it would be good for them to feel like they are part of a community project and are appreciated. With a covered dish lunch planned, it would be nice if the youngsters could be fed and made to feel part of the community spirit which I see as a healthful adjunct for the youngsters, many of whom do not have or get much direction or appreciation from their limited family units."

But the judge's draftees were only part of the workforce. Instead of a few dozen volunteers, the effort attracted a few hundred. And as the number of people interested in participating grew, so did the list of potential projects. The to-do list included reroofing three forty-foot buildings, refurbishing a gymnasium, creating a quarter-mile running track and completely irrigating and landscaping the station grounds.

The Post Office Arcade. *Sandra Thurlow photo collection.*

The event was scheduled for October 8, 1983. Volunteers began showing up before dawn that day, finding different workstations marked with colored balloons. R.L. Brady, a tree surgeon, showed up to help with the landscaping work. Elected officials—including state representative Jim Hill and Martin County commissioners Sherri King and Maggy Hurchalla—pitched in alongside their constituents.

The way Jefferson described it later, the day unfolded a bit like the scene in the Bible when Jesus took a few fish and scraps of bread and turned it into a meal big enough to feed the multitudes. The event organizers put out the call for food, and people answered.

"When 400 people showed up to volunteer, we had no idea how to give them lunch," Jefferson recalled. "One of the radio people said what we were doing and food began to appear. One man brought a canoe full of ice and people began to fill it with salads. Ladies arrived with cakes and other desserts. Restaurants and grocery stores sent food. We fed everyone."

According to news reports, McDonald's and Jake's Restaurant were among the local businesses providing food, which included hamburgers, hot dogs and an assortment of covered dishes.

At the end of the day, after all the work had been completed, Manatee Resort & Marina opened its doors for a "celebration party" for participants.

The original goal had been to save about $75,000 in city funds. However, the *Vero Beach Press-Journal* calculated the volunteers worked a combined 5,400 hours. At the federal minimum wage rate of $3.35 per hour, that translated into more than $18,000 in labor costs alone, not to mention the materials and other in-kind services to support the effort.

Not only did the work get done, but Jefferson also remembered the residual feelings of goodwill that lingered after the event was over. "Afterwards, the police told me that for weeks they would not stop a truck for fear that they had participated in Community Service Day," Jefferson said. "I often wonder what would have happened if it rained that day."

But it didn't.

The volunteers were recognized in a full-page ad in the *Palm Beach Post* on November 3, 1983.

There was at least one unhappy footnote: Jefferson sent a letter to Thomas Weber, editor of the *Stuart News*, criticizing what she considered to be the newspaper's sparse coverage of the event. She also chastised the *Stuart News* for publishing a photo of a pile of trash near the site of the event that apparently was unrelated to the community's cleanup work. Jefferson apparently was pretty steamed because, long before this became a common practice on social media, she typed the November 18, 1983 letter to Weber in all-caps to underscore her point.

Had circumstances been different, Stuart's Community Service Day might have become an annual event. The timing wasn't quite right for that, though.

"I did not think about organizing another Community Service Day, because Peter and I were going on sabbatical in 1984 and I would be leaving the commission," Jefferson recalled.

Instead, with Joan Jefferson's term on the commission over, she and Peter spent 1984 visiting every state in the United States in Carrot, their motor home.

In the Jeffersons' absence, apparently no one thought to keep the Community Service Day going.

It did serve its purpose. Not only were some much-needed improvements made, but city residents also got a chance to see what was possible when they all worked together. "It was magic," Joan Jefferson said decades later.

And it was the kind of magic that would be needed, time and time again, throughout the late 1980s and early 1990s when Stuart's downtown revitalization really began in earnest.

Chapter 5

NEED FOR NEW JAIL SPARKS DEBATE ABOUT DOWNTOWN'S FUTURE

As previously mentioned, downtown was struggling during the early part of the 1980s. Businesses were closing or leaving the central city area in favor of strip shopping centers and malls stationed along busy roadways in outlying neighborhoods. As a result, there were fewer and fewer reasons for other people to go there.

However, the downtown jail was still attracting plenty of "tenants," even if they weren't there by choice. A few former inmates filed a federal lawsuit complaining about overcrowded conditions at the jail. The county had built a temporary stockade to help manage the influx of inmates, but that, too, quickly reached its capacity. New sentencing guidelines required the jail to hold prisoners for longer periods of time, which led to problems when new inmates arrived.

By 1984, Martin County commissioners were ready to build a new jail to address the overcrowding problems identified in the lawsuit. It would prove to be a task more easily said than done.

And discussions about the new jail's location would trigger a series of events that helped define the debate about downtown's future.

Building a new jail at a different location was one option under consideration. But there were other possibilities to consider. The discussion broadened to include other government buildings that could be relocated and/or rebuilt near the new jail.

One option was building a new jail, courthouse, sheriff's office and county administration building all at what was known as the Sailfish Park site off

Flagler Street. Another choice was building the new jail and courthouse at Flagler Street but putting the sheriff's office and the county administration building at a site on Indian Street, well outside downtown. Or the courthouse and jail could be built on Flagler, with the administrative offices at the AmeriFirst building on Southeast Monterey Road, also outside downtown. Or commissioners could relocate all the facilities to either the Indian Street or Monterey Road sites.

Most of the options were expected to cost about the same, between $23 million and $25 million, although relocating everything to Monterey Road was expected to cost closer to $30 million.

One of the main concerns about building at the existing downtown site was there wouldn't be enough available land for expansion as the jail's needs continued to grow.

However, some Stuart residents were worried moving the jail, courthouse or any of the other offices outside downtown would hasten the declining neighborhood's demise. If those government workers left downtown, it would hurt the shops and businesses located there.

In the December 14, 1984 editions of the *Palm Beach Post* and *Miami Herald*, Mayor Stu Hershey was quoted outlining his concerns to the Martin County Commission. "The county is growing south and west, but it's also growing to the north," the *Post* quoted him as saying. "What would you accomplish if you devastate downtown?"

His published remarks in the *Herald* were similar. "I think it's essential the courthouse remain downtown," he said in the *Herald*'s report. "What would be accomplished by building a courthouse elsewhere and leaving Stuart with a dying and decaying downtown?"

By then, the state Department of Corrections had told county officials they needed to come up with steps to address the jail's overcrowding issues by January 10, 1985—which was less than a month away. Otherwise, the county faced the prospect of further legal action being taken by the state attorney general.

Martin County sheriff James Holt took the position that the jail and courthouse needed to be as close together as possible, for the sake of operating efficiency. "The closer to the courthouse, the better off we would be," Holt told commissioners, according to the December 14, 1984 *Post* article. "Our main transactions are there."

One of the commissioners, Maggy Hurchalla, was insistent all of the government offices and the jail should remain part of the same complex. "We should have a unified site with room for expansion," she said in the

Martin County Courthouse, 1925. *Martin County Library System.*

Post article. "If nothing else, our studies have told us about the costs of dividing facilities."

At the December 13 meeting where Hershey spoke, county commissioners voted 4–1, with Hurchalla dissenting, to build a new courthouse next to the existing site but to consider other locations for the new jail. That was far from the last word on the subject.

The next month, the Stuart-Martin County Chamber of Commerce's legislative affairs committee went on record in favor of relocating the courthouse to a spot on US 1, between Indian Street and Cove Road, south of downtown.

"Downtown Stuart won't be losing an ally," committee chairman Bill Hannah said in the January 11, 1985 edition of the *Post.* "It will be losing a nuisance."

The committee unanimously stood behind that recommendation, arguing a new courthouse could create more parking and traffic problems downtown.

At that point, the chamber's board of directors had taken no official position on the relocation plans.

Hannah vowed to lead the charge to move the offices outside downtown, even if he had to do so without the business organization's blessing. "If the board says I can't represent the chamber, I will be at a county commission meeting representing myself and a group of people," Hannah vowed.

Rather than focus on keeping government offices downtown, Hannah suggested forming a downtown revitalization committee. "A revitalization program can create a wonderful shopping center [downtown]," he said.

In a February 14, 1985 letter to the *Stuart News*, Joan Jefferson argued that relocating the courthouse would indeed take care of downtown's parking problem—by emptying the neighborhood out completely. She wrote about how Fort Lauderdale developed "ghetto conditions" in part of its downtown after government offices there were moved. Moving the courthouse toward Martin County's projected population center outside downtown Stuart made as much sense to her as it would to relocate the White House from Washington, D.C., to somewhere in Iowa. "Stuart is, and should be, the heart of Martin County," she wrote.

She added the city's comprehensive plan called for a "vital" downtown that would offer a full range of services to local residents. "This hope trembles on the verge of reality," she wrote.

(Decades later, Jefferson recalled someone brought a casket to one of the many meetings held about the courthouse's future, "to show what would happen to downtown" if it were located elsewhere.)

Others in the community were starting to come around to Jefferson's point of view.

By then, downtown had suffered some serious setbacks, including Florida Power & Light leaving its offices in the historic Post Office Arcade building and the closure of the Stuart Department Store. The merchants who remained downtown had started fighting back by sprucing up the business district with fresh paint and attractive landscaping. Also, entrepreneurs were converting some of the older houses on the western outskirts of downtown into restaurants and professional offices. It was a pivotal time when downtown's fortunes seemed like they could go in either a negative or positive direction.

Ned Kenna, owner of Triangle Lounge and Discount Liquors, told the *Miami Herald* it would be "a travesty" if the courthouse were moved outside downtown. "Of course, the Triangle will survive no matter what," Kenna said in the *Herald*'s February 14, 1985 edition. "But downtown needs the good guys, the bad guys, the lawyers, the stenographers. We just need these people."

That month, county officials were weighing ten options for a government complex, excluding the courthouse and jail, that ranged in projected costs

Coventry House, February 12, 2009. *Sandra Thurlow photo collection.*

from $25 million to $35 million. City officials weren't willing to relocate some ball fields at Sailfish Park, near the proposed downtown site, to some property the YMCA owned on Monterey Road because the county didn't want to pay the relocation cost.

New mayor Pete Walson complained the city was being "jerked around" by the county over the courthouse site. "I find it hard to talk about it, because frankly, I'm mad as hell," Walson said.

Another sticking point was the city's unwillingness to relocate its sewer plant from East Ocean Boulevard to allow more room for a new courthouse and expanded jail. Commissioners said moving the treatment plant would be cost prohibitive. "It would be much easier to move the whole town of Stuart than to move the sewer plant," City Commissioner Charles Foster said.

The political winds began to swirl in March 1985. Three of the five county commissioners had signaled a willingness to keep the courthouse downtown, provided the jail was built on another site.

The pro-downtown courthouse faction was beginning to mobilize, too. About twenty-five downtown merchants held a rally on March 16, 1985, asking for both the courthouse and the jail to remain downtown at the existing site at 100 East Ocean Boulevard. Keeping the facilities there would save between $4.5 million and $8.5 million over other potential sites.

Three days later, the *Stuart News* outlined the terms of a deal that had been struck between city and county leaders: The city would pay one-quarter of the cost of moving Sailfish Park from 8.9 acres downtown to 20.19 acres off Monterey Road, with the county covering the balance of the relocation costs. The county had recently acquired the Monterey Road property from the YMCA, so relocating the park seemed like a solution that would create a bigger footprint for a new courthouse and jail downtown.

By that point, the Department of Corrections had followed through on its threat to cite both the jail and temporary stockade for overcrowded conditions, so pressure was building to get something done.

Then came what would later be referred to as "the yellow ribbon meeting."

On March 19, 1985, about 160 people packed the commission meeting chambers, most of them downtown courthouse supporters who wore yellow ribbons as a show of unity. Their numbers included many attorneys who spent much of their time at the courthouse.

Julie Preast, a downtown business owner, recalled the meeting chambers "was standing room only. The room was packed with people."

One of the leaders of the group, an attorney named Doug Sands, presented commissioners with a petition signed by 1,473 people who wanted to keep the courthouse downtown. Earlier that day, the Stuart-Martin County Chamber of Commerce's board of directors had ended its neutrality by voting in support of a downtown location. Many of the merchants weren't satisfied with only the courthouse and jail staying downtown. They wanted all of the government offices to remain there.

Commissioners didn't give them everything they wanted. At that night's meeting, the commission voted to build an $8.3 million courthouse at the 100 East Ocean Boulevard site, where the courthouse had been located for sixty years. But commissioners left the door open to building the jail somewhere else. That displeased Commissioner Hurchalla, who said it was important to keep the jail and courthouse together.

Sheriff Holt didn't seem to have a location preference—"Just give me enough room," he told commissioners—although he expressed a dislike for multilevel jails, which he felt were harder to manage.

Even though merchants didn't get a commitment to keep all of the offices downtown, the commission's decision to keep the courthouse there was viewed as a key victory. "We pushed and pushed, and they ended up voting to keep the building down there," downtown business owner Jim Dirks said, decades later.

This particular courthouse drama hadn't fully played itself out, though.

In January 1986, county commissioners promised the Department of Corrections and a federal judge the new jail would be built in about fifteen months. They had identified a forty-acre site off Cove Road but backed away from that choice after Sheriff Holt voiced his opposition. Without the chief lawman's support, commissioners weren't sure they would have enough political support for a public referendum on jail construction.

The number of potential sites by this point had grown to thirteen.

Then on February 5, 1986, the *Miami Herald* reported that commissioners had finally decided to build a new jail next to the new courthouse, with a smaller jail annex for minimum-security inmates north of Indiantown. In doing so, commissioners rejected a plan to build the main jail about fifteen miles west of Stuart. There was pressure to get moving on the work because the jail needed to be under construction by mid-1987 to avoid a potential takeover by the federal government.

"For three years now, the idea of a new jail has circled like a large predatory bird over Martin County, threatening to land first here, then there," the *Herald* wrote.

Controversy lingered.

On March 13, 1986, the *Martin County News* reported about twenty East Stuart residents were protesting against putting a new jail at the downtown site. "I live in East Stuart and nobody wants a jail in their backyard," City

First St. Lucie Annex, January 15, 2003. *Sandra Thurlow photo collection.*

Commissioner James Christie Jr. said in the *News* article. "But I've worked hard to keep the courthouse and other governmental units downtown and I feel I must continue my support."

In June of the following year, with construction well underway, the county commission fired Federal Construction Co., the courthouse project's main contractor, for failing to secure a bond for the project, as required by law.

Nevertheless, despite those hiccups, the new Martin County Courts and Constitutional Offices Complex opened at 100 East Ocean Boulevard thirty-nine days ahead of schedule and $225,000 under budget, the *Stuart News* reported on January 10, 1989.

"It's a dream come true," Martin County Circuit Court clerk Marsha Stiller said in the January 8, 1989 issue of the *Palm Beach Post*.

A few years later, the new courthouse was diagnosed with "sick building syndrome" and temporarily closed until dangerous molds could be removed. But the long-running debate about where to put the new jail and courthouse was finally settled.

What to do about the old courthouse building was a separate issue that would be debated as other steps were being taken to revitalize downtown.

Chapter 6

DANCIN' THE BLIGHT AWAY

I
t's impossible to solve a problem until you're willing to admit you have a problem," the old adage goes.

And that's how it was for Stuart city officials as they mulled over ways to improve downtown during the mid-1980s. By then, they realized the neighborhood was in need of some outside help.

The state had a process for allowing local governments to designate neighborhoods as "community redevelopment areas." This involved setting up a local community redevelopment agency, which would have authority to buy and sell land, negotiate deals with developers and establish special taxing districts. Stuart city commissioners were interested in having those tools available to aid their redevelopment efforts, but there was a catch. In order for a neighborhood to be designated as a redevelopment area, it first had to be declared "a slum" or "blighted." That was not a step that sat well with some of the city's boosters, who thought such a declaration would cast a dark cloud over the city's image.

"Red flags went up," downtown business owner Julie Preast said.

At a city commission meeting in July 1985, a representative from the Florida League of Cities tried to downplay the stigma of applying the term "blighted" to downtown. About forty cities in the state had already made similar designations to qualify for state funding and assistance, Ann Jenkins, the league's intergovernmental programs coordinator, told commissioners.

"It's really just a way of saying things are going downhill, or maybe that nothing is happening and there's a need to improve things," Jenkins was quoted as saying in the July 25, 1985 edition of the *Stuart News*.

At a meeting the following month, the city commission reluctantly declared downtown blighted. That made it possible to establish the Stuart Community Redevelopment Agency, which still exists at this writing and has been responsible for funding and managing many of downtown's improvements through the decades.

Thomas Weber, the former *Stuart News* editor, said setting up a taxing district was an indication of just how serious downtown's issues had become and how much merchants and other local residents wanted to fix them. "I was taken by it, as I recall," Weber said. "People don't normally vote to tax themselves unless they are really motivated. There wasn't hardly anyone piqued about it."

Getting Stuart designated as a participant in the state's Main Street program was another key step. Many cities around the country have Main Street programs now, but back then, it was a newer idea. Stuart's leaders didn't warm up to it until 1987, and it took some financial and political wrangling to get them there.

"Downtown Stuart can become a showplace again, if good ideas are reinforced by hard work," the *Stuart News* wrote in a February 6, 1987 editorial arguing in favor of establishing a Main Street program.

The original motivation for Stuart starting a Main Street program was pretty simple: city leaders were hoping to get a $575,000 grant. A consultant

Hawken House, January 15, 2003. *Sandra Thurlow photo collection.*

told them that becoming a Main Street city could improve the odds of getting that grant. That was the expected short-term benefit. Over the long term, being part of the program was expected to help the city qualify for other types of grants and get technical assistance from the state's experts in downtown revitalization.

There was, however, the matter of a $25,000 application fee, which wasn't easy for the city to scrape together. Downtown supporters passed the hat and received donations from many local residents. One of the highest profile among them was Frances Langford, a singer and actress known for entertaining military troops with Bob Hope. Langford and her husband, Ralph Evinrude, head of the well-known boat manufacturer, lived in Jensen Beach and had a reputation for making philanthropic contributions to various local causes.

The couple also happened to be friends of the Jeffersons. This was evident when Joan Jefferson sent letters of thanks to Langford and others who gave significant donations toward the application fee. "It struck me that it might be an appropriate time to thank you on a community level for the many contributions (both personal and financial) that you and Ralph have given over the years, and on a personal level for encouraging Peter and I to move to Stuart 20 years ago, and letting us stay in your villa until we could find a place to live," Jefferson wrote in the February 10, 1987 letter to "Mrs. Ralph Evinrude."

Even contributions from Langford and other benefactors weren't quite enough, though. The city had raised $23,000 through its fundraising drive, but the *Stuart News* reported it took an eleventh-hour assist from the Community Redevelopment Agency to cover the balance needed.

The city's bid wasn't guaranteed once the fee was paid. There was a competitive process to get accepted as a part of the statewide program.

Jim Dirks, a downtown businessman who represented the city during the application process, said nine cities made pitches to Main Street's statewide organization at a meeting in Tampa that year.

In March 1987, the state approved Stuart's application to join the program. According to the *Palm Beach Post*, the city's application was ranked fifth among the nine that were submitted. That was good enough.

Stuart officials took advantage of the new designation to get grants to pay for assorted expenses, including coral-colored sidewalks and tests to find sewer line leaks.

Managing the city's Main Street program wasn't without its challenges. The city hired Donna Renninger to oversee the program, but her tenure there was short and tumultuous. Renninger frequently complained that the city wasn't doing enough to support the Main Street program, which Jefferson and others disputed. Main Street programs typically rely on a blending of government funding and contributions from local businesses.

A November 19, 1987 article in the *Martin County News* seemed to support Renninger's contention about the city. According to the article, Stuart's city government was spending less on its Main Street program than any of the other four newly minted Main Street cities.

The *Martin County News* reported Stuart's Community Redevelopment Agency had provided the city Main Street program with only $2,100, while other cities were contributing from $15,000 to $30,000 toward their programs. "I don't know why we receive less than other cities," Renninger told the newspaper. "I don't think our city realizes how the other cities are financed."

By the program's second year of operations, the *Stuart Mirror* reported it was $36,000 short of what it needed to continue its operations.

By August 1988, Renninger was on her way out as Main Street's manager.

Sally Swartz, a columnist for the *Palm Beach Post*, wrote what amounted to Renninger's parting shots in a piece published on October 4, 1988. Renninger said her greatest failure was failing to establish a collaborative relationship with city commissioners. "The city and the downtown merchants didn't understand what the Main Street program was all about," Renninger said in Swartz's column. "It was difficult to educate them."

Renninger didn't stop there. She also took the city to task for failing, in her mind, to adequately plan for downtown's needs. "It would have helped if the city had a plan for redevelopment," Renninger said. "If they had known what they wanted to do."

Renninger abruptly left the program after it was unable to raise enough money to cover her salary.

Decades later, Joan Jefferson remembered Donna Renninger's time with Main Street a bit differently. "Donna did not meet with any of the commission or staff and began her job by criticizing most actions taken by the commission and castigating us because she broke a heel from her shoe while crossing the railroad tracks," Jefferson emailed in response to questions about Renninger.

Jefferson said she couldn't recall the details of the heel-breaking incident, but apparently it was related to the condition of downtown streets and left the Main Street director with an unfavorable early impression of Stuart. That didn't endear her to Jefferson or her colleagues on the commission.

Lady Abundance. *Sandra Thurlow photo collection.*

"We refused to support [Renninger] and agreed to provide no funding for Main Street," Jefferson recalled. "Because of lack of funding, she had to leave. The next Main Street manager started by meeting with the commission and staff and asked how she could overcome our distaste for Main Street. With a partner instead of an adversary, we began to fund Main Street and had many successful years in the partnership."

(Years later, Jefferson would demonstrate her personal commitment to Main Street by moving to Tallahassee to oversee the statewide organization's operations.)

Nancy Sailer, a longtime community activist, said it was true Stuart city government provided less funding for its Main Street program during its early years than some other communities. And that was an obstacle. "We were struggling," Sailer said. And because of Main Street's struggles, it was tough to convince local businesses to get involved and contribute some of their money to the program.

The downtown merchants had their own association, which led some of them to question the need for a separate Main Street organization. There was also the Downtown Redevelopment Agency, which City Commissioner James Christie had suggested in 1985. With multiple groups involved, downtown business owner Jim Dirks said "there was push and pull" about which entity should be paying for various improvements.

A big turning point in the Main Street group's history occurred in 1988, when it organized a fundraiser that eventually became known as "Dancin' in the Streets." Expectations were fairly low. There seemed to be a number of factors working against the inaugural event's success. For one thing, it was going to be held in August, when, in Dirks's words, "it was hot as hell."

Even Jefferson, one of downtown's biggest boosters, had her doubts about the event's timing. She expressed them to Ann MacMillan, a downtown business owner who was one of the lead organizers. "When she [MacMillan] told me she was going to do this, I said, 'You're going to dance in the streets in the middle of August, and you expect anybody to come?'" Jefferson recalled.

"Absolutely," MacMillan replied.

MacMillan said holding the event in August made sense because it was a time when children were out of school for the summer.

Weather was seen as a potential obstacle for another reason. Sailer said there was also a threat of rain the first year, which nearly forced the event's cancellation. The organizers decided to take a chance anyway.

They rounded up five bands who were willing to play, for free, at the inaugural event. The back of a flatbed truck was pressed into service as a makeshift stage, with a parachute stretched over it to provide some shade. Sailer said extension cords were run from nearby shops on Flagler Avenue and Osceola Street to supply electricity for the sound equipment.

There was no admission charge the first year. The merchants were hoping to make whatever money they could for the Main Street program through concession sales.

It turned out they could make a lot.

"We ran out of beer around 9:30 or 10," Sailer said. "My point is, we got people downtown."

Despite the weather and the unsophisticated trappings, the street festival was a big hit with local residents, who were happy to have an excuse to be downtown again. MacMillan said she was picking up garbage the morning after the event when a man in a pickup truck stopped to personally thank her.

Other residents were grateful, too. "There had never been anything like this downtown," Sailer said. "The first year was such a novelty."

The festival raised about $15,000, which was far more than anyone had expected. Sailer said it helped that the bands performed for free the first year. That wasn't true in the subsequent years of the festival's operations. Also, some of the proceeds came from a raffle, which Sailer said was a tradition that wasn't continued after the first year.

One fundraiser wasn't enough to snap the Main Street group out of its financial doldrums, though. In a January 5, 1989 *Stuart News* article, Jefferson called for Main Street, the Community Redevelopment Agency and the City Commission to work together on a cooperative strategy. It would happen eventually, but not without some further growing pains along the way.

According to the January 11, 1989 minutes from Main Street's board of directors meeting, there was still much concern about media reports on the group's finances. "The board discussed the fact that M.S.'s [Main Street's] financial straits were played up too much in newspaper stories, and that in the future its accomplishments should be stressed," the minutes read.

The financial straits were about to improve, thanks to the group's newly discovered fundraising ability. That first street festival was the beginning of a tradition that lasted for decades. "Every year, it started to snowball," Dirks said. In addition to bands performing, Dancin' in the Steets included other activities, like kids' games and dancing contests.

One of the key catalysts in those early years was Bernie Malone, who became the festival's hard-charging director. Malone was a fixture on event days, often seen with a backpack and cargo shorts stuffed with cash raised from the increasingly larger crowds. "He was in your face," Dirks said of Malone. "He was one of those type of people."

The festival eventually got to a point where it was generating about $65,000 to $70,000 annually, making it Main Street's main fundraiser. The festival's success invigorated local merchants, who took turns providing whatever help was needed. Thomas Weber, the former *Stuart News* editor, noted the festival required a lot of cooperation and coordination on street closures and many other details.

It was hard to argue about the payoff, though. "They [the festivals] really energized the place," Weber said.

The merchants had good reason to root for the festival's success. Festivalgoers frequently did some shopping during their downtown visits. Dirks said it wasn't unusual to have one thousand people visit his business on festival days. "Everybody worked very hard," he said.

Sailer said Dancin' in the Streets became a cause merchants could rally behind, following years of individual business owners focusing primarily on protecting their own interests. "They had to work together, the merchants and Main Street," Sailer said.

It wasn't always smooth sailing. By 1990, the Downtown Business Professional Association, which had a mission similar to Main Street's, had

Dyer Building, February 12, 2009. *Sandra Thurlow photo collection.*

been disbanded. That left some business owners feeling they no longer had a strong advocate to fight for their agenda.

"Since the DBPA was dissolved, the merchants [*sic*] problems and concerns seems [*sic*] to have been put on the back burner," the minutes from the January 10, 1990 Main Street board meeting read. "It is now time to examine where we are and where we are headed."

In a November 30, 1990 editorial, the *Palm Beach Post* encouraged downtown merchants and residents to get along. One source of the friction was so much money was being spent downtown by that point that some residents felt like other parts of the city weren't getting adequate attention. It turned out to be a minor speed bump on downtown's road to revitalization.

Dancin' in the Streets prompted the merchants to begin hosting other events throughout the year, including Friday Night Live, Fashion Catastrophe, the Halloween Monster Mash, the Rocky Horror Picture Show, Christmas Southern Style, the Soroptimist Parade and ArtFest. As the money from those fundraisers started coming in, Dirks said it was easier for local residents to buy into the idea that the Main Street program was worth having. "It made things so much better, so much easier for all of us," Dirks said.

Sailer suggested the program's early struggles were actually beneficial in the long run. "What we went through made us a stronger and a better Main Street," Sailer said.

There were only twenty-five businesses located downtown in 1987. By 1992, there were eighty-seven. Downtown's building occupancy rate reached 100 percent by 1995, up from 20 percent in 1986, according to a *Palm Beach Post* article. By then, the questions were not about whether Main Street had enough money to survive but whether the organization had become too politically powerful.

Given where downtown had been, it was a nice problem to have.

Chapter 7

SWEATING THE SMALL STUFF

S aving downtown Stuart wasn't only a matter of keeping a few historic buildings functional or planning new developments to bring more people to the neighborhood, although that was certainly part of the recipe. A big part of getting people to return to downtown involved making small changes to improve its visual appeal.

Beautification efforts weren't a new phenomenon that began during the 1980s. There were people committed to making the town look better dating at least back to Edwin A. Menninger, if not further back in time. Menninger, a journalist who eventually became owner and publisher of the *Stuart News*, arrived in Florida in 1922 and was disappointed by the lack of flowering vegetation he saw. "Ponce de Leon was dreaming when he called this place Florida, the land of flowers," Menninger was quoted as saying in a February 22, 1982 *Stuart News* historical article. "There weren't any."

Menninger, who became known as the "Flowering Tree Man," made it his life's work to plant flowering trees throughout the city. He was so dedicated to that purpose that the Menninger Flowering Tree Conference for botanists and horticulturalists was named in his honor and he was recognized by the Florida Federation of Garden Clubs. A park on East Ocean Boulevard, a few blocks east of downtown, bears his name.

The city also had a beautification committee that was in operation at least as early as 1980. However, it wasn't until the 1980s that the committee's work seemed to gain some traction.

Lyric Theatre. *Sandra Thurlow photo collection.*

In its battle to stave off the malls and shopping centers in outlying neighborhoods, downtown's historic shopping district had a couple of advantages. One was the comparatively low cost of rents. According to a January 3, 1982 *Stuart News* article, downtown rents were running about five to seven dollars per square foot, compared to twelve to sixteen dollars per square foot in nearby malls. Downtown merchants could also boast of parking closer to their shops, which made loading purchased goods into cars much easier.

However, in the same article, Ann MacMillan, who was then spearheading the Downtown Beautification Committee with former shop owner Marsha Hupfel, complained many downtown buildings had absentee owners and the owners their group were able to contact weren't necessarily committed to spending money on aesthetic improvements. "What we need is cooperation," MacMillan said.

Even simple touches, like planters filled with flowers, could be a source of controversy. "That was our first attempt at beautification," said MacMillan, who owned the Pipette children's clothing store. "We started with planters."

At the time she bought her store, MacMillan said the previous owner was concerned about the city's plans for "bulb-outs," planters that extended into the street. "That meant they would be taking a parking space for each of those bulb-outs," MacMillan said. "And he [the previous owner] was very upset that they were taking parking away from the retailers. But yet, it was part of beautification that had already been started just before I took ownership." At this writing, some of those bulb-outs remain along Flagler Avenue and Osceola Street.

As noted in the previous chapter, setting up the redevelopment district and Main Street program gave downtown boosters new sources of income to pay for improvements. "That gave them money to redevelop the sidewalks," former *Stuart News* editor Thomas Weber said. "They had other things they needed to pay for. The taxing district helped pay for that. It really impressed me."

Yet where to put improvements like landscaping features without interfering with commerce was a source of tension throughout the 1980s and beyond. In a January 3, 1982 *Stuart News* article, for example, "Mrs. Robert Means" of Means Jewelry Store suggested planters near parking spaces on Osceola needed to be removed. "I think the planters are a wonderful idea, but I would like to see them against buildings or on walkways where there is more than adequate room for them," Means said.

Earl Dyer Ricou, owner of Ricou Photo Sports, suggested hanging flowerpots from light poles or placing them in moveable planters. He clearly wasn't crazy about having them on the sidewalks outside shops. "I think these flower beds are for the birds," Ricou said in the newspaper article. "They take up at least a dozen parking spaces."

Nancy Sailer, who worked for the Stuart-Martin County Chamber of Commerce, was in the pro-planter faction. "We did some landscaping that took up some parking spaces, but it added [beauty]," Sailer said. "It looked so much prettier."

Much of the landscaping was on Osceola, considered the shopping district's "inside street."

Even small improvements were starting to make a difference. In a February 18, 1982 editorial, the *Stuart News* commented on the progress that had been made in sprucing up downtown's appearance. "Stuart's downtown is a far more attractive place than it was only two years ago," the newspaper wrote.

Jim Dirks, the owner of Stuart Stained Glass, noted there were always discussions about balancing street improvements with the need for parking. "Parking has been an issue all along," said Dirks, who has since moved his shop outside the downtown core area. "Back when I was there, we were just hoping for a parking space."

Preast said many ideas to improve the parking situation were discussed through the years. "They considered building a garage," Preast said. "They considered buying vacant land to put parking on it. Those types of things were under discussion."

One of the ideas was to provide free valet parking for downtown shoppers. However, for whatever reason, that idea didn't pan out.

There was also talk, at various times, about waiving a city ordinance that required new developments to provide at least one parking space for every one hundred feet of floor space inside their buildings. That might have helped more if there had been room to construct more new buildings downtown. Given that downtown was essentially built out by the 1980s, and the challenge was filling the existing buildings with owners/tenants, that solution didn't provide much relief as shoppers started to return downtown.

There was even debate about whether shoppers should be allowed to use the parking lot outside Stuart City Hall. City Manager Ed Glasscock pushed back against that suggestion, saying those parking spaces were needed to accommodate city employees. "There aren't enough spots for people coming to business with the city," he was quoted as saying in the January 3, 1982 edition of the *Stuart News*.

Railroad tracks run through the heart of downtown, parallel to the historic district's Flagler Avenue. Florida East Coast Railway also owned some of the land adjacent to the tracks, which was used for public parking.

Relations between the city and the railroad seemed to be at a low ebb in 1985, when Florida East Coast wanted to increase the amount it was charging the city to use the railroad right of-way land from a token $1 per year to about $4,000 annually.

The city had been paying a dollar a year since the mid-1920s. Since the city took responsibility to keep the property it used for parking maintained, the arrangement had seemingly suited both sides for decades, until FEC decided to increase the rates in 1985. When the city refused to pay the increased rent, the railroad used barricades to block off its property from public use. In an October 30, 1985 *Stuart News* article, then–city manager Robert McGrath accused the railroad company of acting "spitefully" and "unprofessionally" by closing off those twenty-five spaces. "There is probably a little bit of spitefulness because the city has not keeled over to their demands," McGrath said.

But FEC president R.W. Wyckoff wasn't ready to back down. "We're obviously protecting our property," Wyckoff told the *News*. "They [the city] gave up on their leases."

Relations with FEC eventually improved.

The February 28, 1989 edition of the *Stuart News* detailed the city's plan to add one hundred parking spaces on railroad land parallel to Flagler between First Street and Confusion Corner. The arrangement was contingent upon FEC's approval, which was granted. Railroad officials also agreed to allow parking as close as 50 feet from crossings, as opposed to requiring a 250-foot buffer.

Dirks, the owner of Stuart Stained Glass, said creating the new spaces between the tracks and Flagler was his idea, even if he didn't get credit for it. "I drew that up back in the mid-1980s," Dirks said. "It's pretty much exactly what's there [at present day]. I drew it up on a piece of paper and handed it to this consultant the city had hired and they couldn't come up with a way of really doing anything."

A couple of months later, Dirks said his idea showed up in a report as one of the consultant's recommendations. "They got paid something like $70,000," Dirks said wryly.

With little touches here and there, the improvements made during the mid- to late 1980s started to add up.

The August 19, 1990 issue of the *Stuart News* included a report about the city putting the finishing touches on a $1.6 million overhaul that included pink sidewalks, brick-accented roadways, landscaping, streetlights and drainage and sewage upgrades. Those renovations had been a source of frustration for some merchants. "I am not sure if they are finished yet," said Russ Long, owner of Accurate Services answering service, in the article. "Every time I think they are, they dig another hole."

Inconveniences notwithstanding, the *Stuart News* had given its blessing to the progress that had been made over the previous decade in an August 10, 1990 editorial. The editorial noted that in 1980, there were some in the community who feared downtown was slipping into a state of "irreversible decline." "Structures were falling into disrepair, some stores stood empty, and business stagnated," the editorial explained. "Back then, not many people complained about a parking shortage downtown, because too few people bothered to go downtown."

As the new decade was dawning, the newspaper noted how much had changed: "Although much remains to be done, at least there is renewed interest in downtown Stuart. Even complaints about insufficient parking can be taken as an indirect compliment. It means more people want to go downtown for business, shopping, dining and entertainment."

It seemed like the days of being able to roll a bowling ball down downtown streets without hitting anyone were over.

Chapter 8

A DOWNTOWN LANDMARK
TAKES CENTER STAGE

The Lyric Theatre, located at 59 Southwest Flagler Avenue in the heart of downtown Stuart historic shopping district, has been an important part of the community's history since the day its doors opened. Like many buildings in the historic district, the theater actually has entrances on both Flagler and Osceola Streets for easy access by patrons.

Judge John Hancock and his wife, Mamie, built the Lyric in 1925 at a cost of $100,000. Although Stuart now has numerous larger buildings, at the time of its construction, the Lyric was the largest building in Martin County, according to historical information on the theater's website. It replaced an earlier version of the theater, with a significantly smaller audience capacity of 250, which had been built on Osceola Street in 1913.

The "new" Lyric was built as a silent movie house with a small stage to accommodate vaudeville acts. It officially opened on March 15, 1926, with Mamie Hancock playing an overture on a pipe organ and a screening of *Skinner's Dress Suit*. According to the theater's account, the first show was a sellout, with people turned away at the front doors.

"Judging from the attendance at theatre, The Lyric is going to be a mighty popular place," the *Stuart News* wrote about opening night. "It is indeed an ideal playhouse and one that every resident of Stuart might well be proud of."

The Lyric became an important gathering place for community events like the screening of *Westward, Ho*, a silent movie filmed in Stuart in 1916.

A few years later, on December 1, 1930, a "talkie" movie, *Danger Lights*, was shown there for the first time. The Lyric survived the transition from silent movies to movies with sound but eventually fell on hard times in the years following the Great Depression.

Through the years, the building's ownership changed hands several times. The building was sometimes rented out for use by community groups. People still came to see traveling vaudeville shows, movies and newsreels there, too.

In 1978, the New Life in Christ Church bought the building and began using it for weekly services. Nine years later, though, the church was interested in relocating and put the building up for sale.

Roy Laycock, a local real estate salesman, saw the Lyric's potential as both a community amenity and a source of civic pride. "He wanted to make sure the theater didn't get changed into an office building or something else," said Richard Geisinger, another local real estate agent and friend of Laycock's.

Laycock believed the Lyric, positioned where it was among the historic district's shops, could help draw more people back to downtown. "The theater is like a major tenant in a strip mall," Geisinger said. "It's the thing you want to pull people downtown. Then they've got to eat, then they've got to shop, all that kind of stuff."

As the story goes, Laycock didn't have enough money to buy the Lyric but entered into negotiations with the church to buy the building anyway. He struck a verbal deal to buy the structure for $300,000. Then he went door to door, seeking $500 contributions from individual donors to cover the $5,000 deposit he needed to secure the deal. He raised enough to cover the down payment but still needed more to cover the balance and retire his debt. He was fortunate in a couple of respects.

For one, he was able to recruit a group of people in the community who shared his vision and formed the Friends of The Lyric, a nonprofit

Lyric Theatre, 1926. *Martin County Historical Society.*

organization to raise funding for the theater's operations. "After he made the deal, he called a bunch of his friends up and said, 'Hey, I've got a contract, this is my idea, and we really need to save this thing,'" Geisinger recalled.

For another, the church was willing to let the new almost-owners use the venue to host fundraisers while the sale was still under contract.

Geisinger was one of the Friends of the Lyric's original board members, who joined those efforts to return the Lyric to its former glory during the 1980s.

Although Laycock got the movement started, he wasn't around to see it through. He moved away from the area, leaving the other board members to figure out how to complete the purchase. "We're like, 'OK, what do we do now?'" Geisinger said. "None of us had any theater experience."

That lack of experience wasn't enough to deter the group's members. "We rolled up our sleeves and started to produce shows," Geisinger said. "It was all hands on deck."

The board members volunteered their time as theater ushers, drink servers, cleaners, painters and repair people. According to the Lyric's website, the building presented many operational challenges. The board members "prayed the restrooms would work when there was a packed house."

There were a lot of lessons the group needed to learn. For example, Geisinger recalled one of the early fundraising shows, involving the band Blood, Sweat & Tears. "I get a call about noon on a Friday that said, 'Blood, Sweat & Tears is here, and they want to know where the load-in guys are,'" Geisinger said. "We didn't even know they needed load-in guys." Geisinger and one of the other board members ended up unloading the band's equipment themselves.

Another one of the bookings during those years was Rita Coolidge, who delivered an emotional performance before a packed house. Nancy Smith, a columnist for the *Stuart News*, recounted the event in a piece published on April 29, 1988. "In the 11½ years I've lived in Martin County, I've never seen as much excitement generated in one building," Smith wrote. "Rita Coolidge set the place on fire."

The crowd's enthusiasm apparently affected Coolidge, too, as her voice caught with emotion as she addressed audience members. "This is the greatest response I've had to a concert since I played in Japan three years ago," Coolidge said. "I think I'll come back next year. No, I know I'll come back next year!"

Smith wrote what she saw at Coolidge's concert was more evidence downtown Stuart was making a comeback. "I took last Friday evening as a brief glimpse at what Stuart's waterfront area could be," she wrote. "Between the Lyric and the plans to revitalize downtown, I see an exciting future for all of us."

It was that kind of energy that helped Geisinger and the other volunteers keep going, even through periods of uncertainty. "We knew we were doing the right thing," Geisinger said. "We just didn't know how to do it."

While the Lyric had beautiful Art Deco architecture, it also had some limitations. The seating capacity was only about six hundred, so it was better suited for intimate performances than large-scale concerts or other events.

Performers frequently commented on the quality of the Lyric's acoustics. Yet because of the theater's proximity to the railroad tracks, it was sometimes necessary to temporarily halt performances when trains were passing through, said downtown business owner Ann MacMillan.

The stage is only twenty-two feet by thirty feet, which isn't a huge amount of performance space. The lack of space backstage was also a challenge, particularly for loading and storing production equipment and props.

Then there was the theater's overall condition, which could best be described as a "fixer-upper" during those early days of the Friends of the Lyric's involvement.

The air conditioning was unreliable. The roof leaked, which was particularly noticeable during one important meeting about downtown's future that will be detailed in the next chapter. And, on at least one occasion, the theater directors' prayers weren't answered to their satisfaction because there was a sewage backup in the restrooms during one of the performances.

The air conditioning issues, in particular, could be a real problem on hot summer nights with hundreds of people packed into the cozy building. "You did not have a happy audience, or a happy performer," Geisinger said.

The local group learned on the fly about who to approach about bookings, as well as what types of acts would consider playing in a venue like the Lyric. In some cases, the Lyric had to settle for performers who had booked shows farther south in places like Miami or Fort Lauderdale but had gaps in their schedules long enough to allow them to make side trips to Stuart.

For example, Coolidge was available for that 1988 concert in Stuart because she had a gig in Miami the following night. "It didn't take too long to figure out we couldn't afford big talent," Geisinger said. "It was a small theater. We had to find medium talent."

While all of those shows were being booked, the Lyric was still moonlighting as a church, with services held on Sundays.

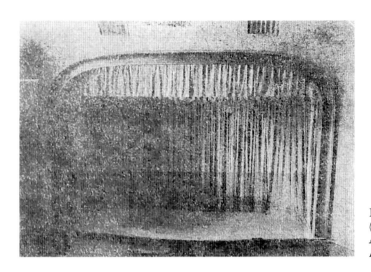

Lyric Theatre
(interior), 1926.
*Martin County
Historical Society.*

The Friends of the Lyric closed on the purchase of the building on March 21, 1988, according to Geisinger.

Maintaining and upgrading the facilities have remained a work in progress since that time. In 1993, for example, a pair of grants and a grassroots fundraising effort paid for repairing the roof, termite spraying, replacing plasterwork, reinforcing stage floors, upgrading wiring and rigging, creating a new projection and control room and other improvements. The building has been renovated and expanded during the three decades that have elapsed since then.

Yet Geisinger is convinced if steps hadn't been taken to preserve the Lyric during the 1980s, its future and the rest of downtown's future might have turned out much differently. "If The Lyric had been purchased [by other buyers] and turned into an office building, I think we would have a different downtown right now," he said. "It could have been a totally different scene. And it would have never been the vibrant place it is now."

Chapter 9

FOUNDERS OF NEW URBANISM
LEND A HAND

In the world of urban design and planning, the names don't get bigger than Andrés Duany and Elizabeth Plater-Zyberk. They are to their chosen profession what Taylor Swift is to music. In a February 21, 1988 article, the *Miami Herald* described the planning power couple as being Napoleon-like in its zeal to remake American cities. More recently, in a May 18, 2010 profile, *The Atlantic* described Duany as "the man who reinvented the city." Not "a" city. Duany and Plater-Zyberk changed a lot of people's ideas about what all modern cities should look like.

They are widely considered to be the founders of New Urbanism, a planning approach that is seen by many as the answer to suburban sprawl. Residential development underwent major changes in the years following World War II. Before the war, most people either lived in cities or in the country. There wasn't much of a middle ground. Then during those postwar years, suburban living began to gain in popularity. A lot of people liked the idea of living near a big city, where they could work and take advantage of the city's amenities, but they wanted to be far enough away from population centers to have less traffic, maybe a little more yard space for their kids and a slower-paced lifestyle.

Suburbs sprouted outside of large and even medium-sized cities, wherever land was available to develop at affordable prices. Housing subdivisions were relatively easy to construct. Quite often, they took a familiar pattern: one or two main roads provided access to the subdivisions. Some were protected by gates and guardhouses; others were not. Within the subdivisions, row after row of houses would be built, usually with similar or even identical styling along winding residential roads that led nowhere. Some subdivisions offered recreational amenities like parks or pools, but usually there was little in the way of commercial development. If people wanted to go shopping or run other errands, most often they would have to get into their cars and drive to wherever they needed to go. In a car-oriented society, it made a lot of sense. For some people, it still does.

But these suburban enclaves had their share of drawbacks. A few years before the 1980s dawned, there was political turmoil in the Middle East, which led to a tremendous spike in gas prices. So-called economy cars became popular in the 1970s as people were looking to stretch what they were spending on gas as far as they could. Still, the way a lot of suburbs were designed, there was no way to avoid getting into the car even for something as simple as a jug of milk or a loaf of bread.

Suburbs were built a distance away from cities to provide residents with a buffer from crime and urban problems. That buffer often was too far to easily traverse on foot or by bicycle. Roads weren't always designed with the safety of walkers or bicyclists in mind, either. That was one practical reason why some homebuyers started looking for alternatives to traditional suburban design.

A less practical but no less important reason was people were growing disenchanted with the type of lifestyle suburban subdivisions offered. Because it was easier for developers to replicate the same type of building styles from project to project, many suburban neighborhoods were indistinguishable from one another. They lacked character. And they lacked an easy mechanism for neighbors to connect with each other.

In the early to mid-twentieth century, city dwellers had opportunities to regularly interact with their neighbors while walking to work or shopping or wherever. Suburban subdivisions, with their reliance on cars as almost the sole form of viable transportation, took away those opportunities. People might know the neighbors next door or within a few doors of where they lived, but the others on nearby streets were strangers they would pass in their cars during their commutes to work.

New Urbanism arose in response to that. Urban planners discovered, in addition to the lifestyle benefits, that it was much more efficient to provide government services like police and fire protection, water and sewer connections and all the rest within compact areas.

"Suburban sprawl" is the term associated with development that extends from urban centers without apparent concern for the strain that places on government resources. Planners took renewed interest in so-called infill developments, which used land already within established urban areas. This was, and still is, known as "smart growth."

As the 1980s began, Duany and Plater-Zyberk were about to take smart growth concepts to a new level.

Duany was the child of Cuban parents who grew up in Barcelona, Spain. Plater-Zyberk came from a Polish family that settled in the Philadelphia suburbs. The couple met as architecture students at Princeton University. Later, they attended graduate studies together at Yale University. They moved to the Miami area in the mid-1970s. Duany worked for a while as a condominium developer before he and Plater-Zyberk formed their own urban planning firm in 1980.

One of their first projects was a master-planned community in the Florida Panhandle that became known as Seaside. Seaside was something new, but it had its roots firmly in the past. It was a community that emphasized the importance of walkability. The streets were narrow, making it safer for people to walk or bicycle along them without fear of being run over by cars. The houses were grouped close together, which made it easier for neighbors to get to know one another. Housing was mixed with commercial development, as it had been in prewar urban areas.

Development within Seaside continued throughout most of the 1980s. Even before the community was built out, it was attracting attention because it was such a different concept for the times. Seaside's quaintness and user-friendliness struck a chord with people who had grown tired of modern suburban and urban lifestyles. Seaside was so idyllic that it was used as a setting for *The Truman Show*, a movie released in 1998 about a man whose life in a near-perfect community is being chronicled in a television show.

In an interview with the *Miami Herald* for a February 21, 1988 article, Duany predicted Seaside would become a model for other communities to copy. "Seaside has no enemies," Duany said, explaining its hallmarks were popular with developers and homebuyers alike. "Within the next 10 years, it will be the next model," Duany said. "All developers will want to copy it." Later in the article, Duany reduced the timeline, saying Seaside's popularity would explode within five years.

Duany was, the *Herald* writer noted, confident to the point of boastfulness. And he wasn't interested in just earning a living in quiet anonymity. "It is not interesting, just to make money," Duany said in the *Herald* article. "What's really interesting is to change the way that America builds itself."

First church, railroad and Stanley Kitching's store, 1890. *Martin County Historical Society.*

Plater-Zyberk lamented that malls were taking the place of traditional downtown areas. And, in her opinion, traditional downtowns were what people really wanted.

The couple wanted to focus on developing in the "classicism" style, building communities that de-emphasized the use of cars, creating town centers and other shared public or semi-public spaces where people could gather within their own neighborhoods. The type of architectural styles used were less important, in their view, than the manner in which neighborhoods or even entire cities were laid out.

Some of their ideas were controversial. For example, rather than allowing free enterprise and individualism to dictate proper development patterns, Duany suggested governments needed to exercise more control over urban planning. "The great capitals of Europe are all due to dictators," Duany said. "Democracy doesn't build the best cities. There's just no doubt about it."

Stuart wasn't run by a dictator in the mid-1980s. However, its city government did have people who were willing to take some risks to reverse decades of declining conditions downtown.

Seaside was, at that point, still a work in progress. But it was a model that caught the attention of the right people in Stuart. The Napoleons of New Urbanism were about to make an entrance.

Chapter 10

HEALTHY HEART, HEALTHY BODY

I n hindsight, it seems unsurprising Duany brought his talents to Stuart. Some of his ideas, like creating live/work spaces with apartments and condominiums located on the upper floors of businesses, meshed with those of Peter Jefferson, Joan's architect husband. And with the early acclaim heaped on Seaside, Duany was a big name within the architectural world, even as far back as the 1980s.

Stuart wasn't the first community in the region to seek out Duany's services, though. Around the same time Stuart officials were getting serious about revamping downtown, Port St. Lucie, Stuart's larger neighbor to the north, was assembling a development plan for the St. Lucie West neighborhood.

The Treasure Coast Regional Planning Council is an organization that provides advice and technical assistance to both communities, as well as others in that part of the state. Dan Cary, the planning council's director, had read articles about Duany's work on Seaside and introduced him to the developer overseeing work on St. Lucie West.

Marcela Camblor, an urban planner who has worked with the planning council, said Duany came up with a plan to bring some of his New Urbanism ideas to St. Lucie West. "It was going to be an amazing new town," Camblor said.

However, the developer died before the plans for St. Lucie West were submitted for government approval. Duany's ideas for St. Lucie West died with him. "[The developer's] heirs decided to stick with a conventional suburban plan," Camblor said.

St. Lucie West could have had a radically different look if the heirs had stuck with Duany's recommendations. Instead, it's largely indistinguishable from the rest of Port St. Lucie, although it does skew a bit more toward commercial development, while other parts of the city are largely residential. "It would have created a culture for more walkable, mixed-use environments, instead of more auto-driven landscapes," Camblor said of Duany's plans for St. Lucie West.

However, through that planning work, Duany had forged a relationship with Cary. When Stuart's leaders were asking for help, Cary suggested Duany might be able to provide it.

Joan Jefferson, who had returned to the Stuart City Commission a year earlier, in 1987, recalled Duany was a bit reluctant to get involved because he was interested in creating entirely new communities, not rebuilding older neighborhoods. "Duany didn't want to come to town," Jefferson said. "He wanted to build new cities. [We said] if this guy is so great, why can't he come to one of our existing communities and apply [his know-how] to an existing community?"

Working in Stuart's favor was Duany's philosophy about the importance of downtown areas to the overall health of their communities. Duany believed that just like a body couldn't function well with an ailing heart, a city couldn't reach its full potential with a substandard downtown, Camblor said.

Jefferson said Duany agreed to consult with Stuart on a design charette, a community-driven planning process, in exchange for a $25,000 fee Carey had offered.

"It was the best thing that ever happened to Stuart," Jefferson said.

Duany's first visit to Stuart in the spring of 1988 didn't seem quite that momentous at the time. In the May 1, 1988 edition of the *Stuart News*, Duany's visit the day before ranked as only the second-most important story of the day, positioned on the front page below a report about the start of sea turtle nesting season. Nevertheless, the *News* reported the audience at the Lyric Theatre was "enthralled" by what Duany had to say.

He warned local residents, in no uncertain terms, their city would either evolve or die. "You know, there isn't a choice," Duany said. "The only way you're going to survive is to radically redesign your cities."

In Duany's mind, that meant creating a more pedestrian-friendly atmosphere. He professed to be "furious at the planning profession" for allowing developers to build unimaginative projects that he didn't feel would stand the test of time. "Planners have control," he said. "They don't have to let developers come up with this. And Stuart really is potentially fabulous. You have to rally people to see that there is a vision."

If you've had experience dealing with government bureaucrats, you might have expected those working for the city to vigorously defend the status quo. Maybe to explain why "the way we've always done it" is the way it should always be.

That's not what happened in this case. Craven Alcott, Stuart's planning and development coordinator, expressed willingness to consider new ideas. "There's room to change," Alcott said. "There's great potential and possibility, and our codes need to be more flexible. We want his creativity, and to take from the best he has."

Duany promised to return in July for a five-day workshop to hash out the details of downtown Stuart's future.

There was a great sense of anticipation within the community in the days leading up to his return visit. The July 3, 1988 edition of the *Stuart News* described it as "the planning blitzkrieg."

To get buy-in for his ideas, Duany would need to unite people with diverse and even sometimes competing interests. For example, within the eighteen blocks designated as the Main Street program's redevelopment area, there were sixty-three different property owners.

Yet there was a high level of trust in Duany's conviction and his interest in doing what he felt was truly best for the community. "Once in a while in your life, you run into people who believe in what they are doing," said Dan Cary, executive director of the Treasure Coast Regional Planning Council, in the *Stuart News* article. "I honestly believe Andrés Duany and his wife are young idealists who believe what they are doing. The reason he's doing it is because he has a strong sense of civic responsibility."

City Commissioner Peter Walson characterized Duany's approach to his work as almost a religious experience. "I'm looking forward to seeing how he will blend the old with the new," Walson said. "He's almost like an apostle of a new wave of thinking about cities. It is professional to him, but it is also personal."

City Commissioner Joan Jefferson said one of Duany's advantages was that he wasn't burdened by a hidden agenda.

"He doesn't have the emotional baggage that we carry," Jefferson said. "Since he doesn't have a vested interest in our community, there won't be any question that he's doing it for this client or that client, or because he wants to build a house on it."

Duany certainly didn't try to sugarcoat the challenges Stuart was facing.

The *Stuart News* ran a follow-up article five days later, headlined "Architects Hit Stuart on Whirlwind," describing espresso-fueled marathon meetings at the City Commission chambers and a makeshift office in the chamber of commerce's old building near Sheppard Park.

"I think there's a very good chance we're going to fail here," Duany told a group of architects at one of the community workshops. "If we don't fail, it will almost be a first."

Whether Duany actually believed that or was just trying to lower expectations is a mystery. When asked about the Stuart planning process decades later, Duany said he could remember few of the details.

However, in the *News* article, Duany said Stuart's downtown had better "fabric" than Miami's renowned Coconut Grove neighborhood. He also said that he thought the meeting with the architects had gone better than it could have. "Only two of them walked out," Duany told the newspaper. "Usually, it's a much higher percentage."

Duany said Stuart needed to have a sense of urgency to avoid the fate that had befallen his adopted hometown of Miami and other major cities. Those cities often lost their vibrancy as suburban development eroded what had made their downtown cores special.

Duany said Stuart's existing set of codes was "a recipe for disaster." "You're on the verge of losing all that you have," Duany said at one of the meetings. "You're going to have the traffic load of a metropolis here and the culture of a rural town, which is the worst of both worlds."

By the end of the weeklong series of meetings, Duany and community leaders seemed much more upbeat. After giving a presentation to local officials on the final night of his tour, Duany asked for questions and was instead met with applause.

"What happened to the angry, incoherent Stuart citizenry?" Duany quipped, according to the July 11, 1988 edition of the *Stuart News*.

Jefferson summed up the excitement about Duany's plans this way: "I am astounded. I am stunned. I am elated. I am optimistic. I am enchanted. I am overwhelmed."

Following those five days of meetings, Duany planned to present his vision during another meeting at the Lyric the following month. It would be a day long remembered by many residents, for many reasons.

It was raining heavily the day of Duany's follow-up presentation. At that point, renovations at the Lyric were a work in progress. One of the areas still in need of improvement was the building's roof, which leaked profusely. Water was dripping on the slide projector Duany was using for his presentation. Richard Geisinger, one of the Lyric's volunteer board members, was so worried the great urban designer might be electrocuted that he left the meeting and took a walk around the block to relieve his stress.

Downtown business owner Ann MacMillan said the rain may have been a distraction, but not enough of one to disrupt the proceeding. The Lyric was "packed" with people (the

Casa Lumber Company, 1925. Stuart News *archives.*

Stuart News estimated the audience at three hundred) from all walks of life, she said. There were builders, developers, planners and other city officials. But there were also teachers, shop owners, people who had little experience with planning and development strategies in their daily lives.

They were eating up what Duany had to say.

"You have everything you need here," Duany told them. "You just need to spruce it up a bit."

MacMillan said Duany's message, and the reception it got from the crowd, clearly marked a turning point in the city's history. "Everybody was in agreement," MacMillan said of the crowd, with many heads nodding in unison. "That's where it started."

If Duany had been pessimistic before about the plan's chances of being implemented, he apparently had a change of heart after seeing how the crowd at the Lyric reacted. "There's very little in-fighting that often leads to these reports turning into nothing," Duany was quoted in the *News* as saying. "It seems that it might really work. The citizens are doers, and the proposals have a chance of being."

Jefferson's enthusiasm hadn't abated in the weeks since Duany's previous visit. "We can do it," she said. "We will do it. I know the people will want to do it."

Following Duany's presentation at the Lyric, the City Commission met later in the day and "conceptually approved" his plans.

Also that day, the Martin County Commission did its part to facilitate one of Duany's recommendations by agreeing to preserve the old courthouse building, while demolishing two wings that had been added years after the main structure was completed in 1937.

"Everything started blowing up at the same time," MacMillan recalled of the momentum following that meeting.

But there was still a lot of work to do. Duany laid out a framework for how downtown Stuart could retain its "old Florida charm," but his plans still had to be successfully executed.

And a lot of what he was suggesting was more easily said than done.

Chapter 11

DUANY'S RECIPE FOR URBAN
SURVIVAL

D uany didn't offer Stuart residents a single magic bullet. It wasn't a case where he thought taking one initiative would be enough to reverse downtown's fortunes. Instead, he proposed a highly detailed plan that included many steps, some seemingly small in scope and others that were fairly momentous.

As previously mentioned, Duany recommended saving the old courthouse, even though the plans already in motion for the new courthouse meant the historic building would need to be used for something other than its original purpose. As part of his overall approach of making communities less car oriented, Duany also recommended moving the parking lot from the front of the courthouse building to the back.

Not everyone thought the old courthouse was worth saving. At the Martin County Commission meeting where the vote was taken to save the original part of the building, local architect Philip Braden described it as "a liability" and "a piece of mediocre art deco," according to the *Stuart News*. Braden derisively suggested that no one seemed to care about the old courthouse's fate until "Andrés Duany, that messiah," recommended saving it.

Duany also advised city leaders to "control the [state] Department of Transportation." At the time, Department of Transportation officials were planning to replace the Roosevelt Bridge, which crossed the St. Lucie River near the heart of downtown, with a new structure that would bypass the central city area. While Duany said the new bridge was "inevitable and possibly necessary," he urged city leaders to keep at least one of the old bridge's twin spans to provide easier access to downtown. "Their removal will turn the downtown commercial streets into a huge cul-de-sac devoid of through traffic," Duany warned.

Duany also opposed the state agency's plan to widen West Ocean Avenue and remove the on-street parking.

The Department of Transportation was also recommending the city "simplify" Confusion Corner, which Duany thought would be counterproductive. Although, true to its name, Confusion Corner could be confusing for some drivers, Duany said, "It is a landmark in Stuart and a symbol of the American Driver when challenged." Instead of replacing the Confusion Corner roundabout with a more conventional street intersection, Duany recommended some beautification work to enhance its status as a local landmark.

"Remember: D.O.T. in its single minded pursuit of traffic flow has destroyed more American Towns than General Sherman," Duany wrote. "This must not happen to Stuart." Duany said, perhaps in jest, that city leaders should consider putting a monument at Confusion Corner, commemorating Stuart's victory over the DOT.

Completely overhauling Stuart's land-use codes was another of Duany's big ideas. He recommended changing the rules to make it easier to accommodate parking behind buildings instead of in front of them, as with the courthouse.

The revised codes also encouraged development of outbuildings, such as mother-in-law apartments or living spaces above shops, to create more opportunities for affordable housing.

The new codes encouraged "traditional" building designs, with features like front porches to foster a greater sense of community.

"When Stuart passes these regulations, it will have among the most sophisticated codes in the world," Duany wrote. "Among American cities, only New York, Washington and San Francisco have comparable documents."

Duany had recommendations for traffic calming, including more street trees and narrow residential streets to discourage, or at least slow down, vehicular traffic. He also suggested concealing a portion of the railroad tracks running through downtown with landscaping.

Duany wanted to demolish the Triangle Lounge and Discount Liquors and put a "pedestrian plaza" in its place in front of city hall. "I hope that

Woodmen Hall, 1914. Stuart News *archives.*

someday it will be an amazing story to tell: that there once was a bar like that in front of City Hall," Duany was quoted as saying in the August 24, 1988 edition of the *Stuart News.*

He also proposed the removal of the Memorial Park bandshell, which he said looked like "a bidet or urinal." Duany recommended an "emerald necklace" of parks throughout downtown.

Duany's plans encouraged construction of townhouses in the old Pottsdam section of downtown, with buildings painted red, cream and ochre colors; arches lining Colorado Avenue and West Ocean Boulevard; and a line of open-air stalls along Flagler Avenue that could be used by vendors at outdoor events.

Duany urged city officials to convince the U.S. Postal Service to open a post office branch downtown. He also urged them to lobby Martin County officials for a branch library downtown.

One of Duany's more unusual ideas was to ban all vending machines downtown. By doing that, Duany reasoned people would spend more money buying food and drink from local merchants.

If you visit downtown Stuart today, you can see some of those recommendations were followed, while others were not. Duany had an idealistic vision for the city. However, there were certain political and practical obstacles that would have to be overcome to implement it.

Downtown Stuart had clearly reached a pivotal moment in its history. Yet there was a lot of work to do.

Chapter 12

KEEPING DOWNTOWN CONFUSING

It wasn't a big surprise that Andrés Duany had ideas about what to do with Confusion Corner as part of his overall plan for revitalizing downtown Stuart. It would have been a lot more surprising if he hadn't.

Confusion Corner is as much a part of Stuart's civic DNA as the Empire State Building is part of New York's or Big Ben is to London's. Just about everybody who has spent any length of time in Stuart has some type of story associated with Confusion Corner.

The name is something of a misnomer. Confusion Corner isn't really a corner at all. It's a roundabout located just south of the historic downtown shopping district, where Flagler Avenue, Ocean Boulevard, Colorado Avenue, Dixie Highway (A1A) and the Florida East Coast Railroad tracks converge.

Confusing, it very much was and is.

Confusion Corner's iconic status was cemented when local musician Clifford Buckosh wrote a song in the 1970s about the driving perils it presented. T-shirts and bumper stickers were available for sale to those who wanted souvenirs of an authentic Stuart experience.

Some drivers have been known to freeze up at the edge of the roundabout, unsure which way they can legally travel. "I can remember a Winnebago could get stuck in there," said Thomas Weber, former editor of the *Stuart News*. "They'd take a wrong turn, then all of the sudden, they couldn't back up."

In a column originally published on April 25, 1978, Weber explained the origin of Confusion Corner, at least as the legend goes. Long before the roads and railroad tracks were built, Confusion Corner was rumored to be the spot where a series of raccoon trails converged. According to Weber's column, the spot was once known as "Raccoon Wash" because the trails ended in a pond that attracted the masked varmints. "I was told the early founders wanted to preserve all the raccoon trails," Weber said in an interview decades later. "That's where they met."

After roads were built, the intersection got its nickname sometime in the 1920s. Through the years, there was talk about making the intersection less confusing. In 1978, for example, the Florida Department of Transportation talked about "fixing" Confusion Corner by installing six traffic lights. That prompted Weber to write his column, which touched on the reason why residents didn't seem anxious to make Confusion Corner more conventional.

In Weber's mind, dealing with traffic at Confusion Corner was an essential skill new residents needed to learn. Having the right temperament was essential to live in Stuart. "It's kind of a test for people who came to town," Weber said in a 2023 interview. "If a person couldn't really deal with the ambiguity that intersection brought up, then they probably didn't belong here. We need people who are a little more easygoing."

In his 1978 column, Weber noted Confusion Corner was prone to traffic backups. When large boats needed to pass downtown along the St. Lucie River, the drawbridge for the old Roosevelt Bridge for cars and the railroad bridge had to be raised. That meant trains had to stop short of the bridge. Some freight trains were long enough to block numerous downtown intersections while sitting idle, including Confusion Corner.

Thus, he wrote, successfully navigating Confusion Corner became a "rite of initiation." "Once a new resident learns to cross the junction without getting sweaty palms, he acquires a sense of native status," Weber wrote. "And so it is we have this intersection to thank for culling out many a misfit who otherwise might have settled in our community. Darwin himself would be impressed with this example of the process of natural selection."

At one point, a garbage can was placed in the middle of Confusion Corner as a marker. Whenever a car hit the garbage can, the can would be moved to a different spot in the intersection. That went on until the can ended up in a spot where it seemed safest from traffic. That became the de facto "center" for the intersection, at least until local residents decided to dress it up and make it a little more decorative.

Aerial photograph, downtown Stuart, circa 1965. *Martin County Library System.*

Community activist Nancy Sailer said the intersection was decorated by a simple flower box for a while. "It had a box and I used to keep flowers in it because I headed up the beautification committee for the chamber [of commerce]," Sailer said. "I would put flowers in the box and the cars would all go by and honk at me."

Jim Dirks, a downtown business owner, said Confusion Corner was considered such a prominent landmark that it was sometimes used as a backdrop for publicity stunts. "I even had friends of mine parachute into Confusion Corner," Dirks said.

According to Dirks, two of his friends left from an airfield in Indiantown on a skydiving excursion that ended in the middle of the intersection. "I don't know how we coordinated it or if we even did, because there were trains going through," Dirks said. "I know we had the police stop traffic."

That and other similar stunts surely attracted some media attention. But Confusion Corner's big break, publicity-wise, was the time when Charles Kuralt came to town. Ann MacMillan said her husband, David, was the one responsible for bringing the national news celebrity to town. The

MacMillans were both fans of Kuralt's program *On the Road*, which featured slices of Americana from around the country. After watching the program one night, Ann said David turned to her and suggested Kuralt should come to Stuart and do a segment on Confusion Corner. "I immediately forgot about it, but he [David] didn't," MacMillan recalled.

David MacMillan either wrote or called CBS to pitch his idea. Kuralt was already in Florida when he got word a doctor from Stuart was trying to get in touch with him. Kuralt called him back, then made plans to do a story on Confusion Corner in 1979. Since the *Stuart News* offices were close to Confusion Corner back then, Kuralt paid a visit to the newsroom to talk with local journalists. "He came and sat with all of us for about five minutes each," Nancy Smith said, recalling the event decades later. "It was a big thrill. He was such a good guy."

At the time, Stuart had seldom, if ever, appeared in a national news broadcast for anything, except perhaps the occasional hurricane passing through the area. (Confusion Corner has continued to get its share of airtime in the years since Kuralt's visit, including an episode of *Expedition Unknown* that aired nationally on the Discovery Channel on August 3, 2022.)

During the traveling journalist's visit to the *News* offices, Smith quizzed Kuralt about his decision to come to town. "I asked him, 'Of all the places you could go, why here?'" Smith recalled. "He said, 'Oh, come on. It's Florida. It's winter. I have choices, but why would I go to Missouri when I can come here?' I think he was honest, too, about that. You could tell he really did like it here."

Kuralt pointed out that watching Confusion Corner traffic had become a spectator sport. "He said, 'There's people on that bench [nearby], just watching the traffic,'" Smith said. "'Where does that happen?'"

Weber said Kuralt had read his column about Confusion Corner from the year before and interviewed him for the news broadcast. "He was the nicest guy in the world, too," Weber said. "I really enjoyed talking to him. Very easygoing."

Ann MacMillan said she and David had dinner with Kuralt and his videographer while they were in town at a restaurant called Lord Chumley's, which is on the site of the present-day Sailor's Return restaurant near the new Roosevelt Bridge. Ann MacMillan remembered how seemingly every patron in the restaurant came over to greet Kuralt that night—and that the newscaster took all the attention in stride.

She also recalled Kuralt's ability to knock back glass after glass of whiskey. "Charles Kuralt could put away the alcohol," MacMillan said. "Then he got up and walked straight out of the restaurant. I asked David: 'How the hell is he walking?' Evidently, he had that reputation."

That was Confusion Corner's first brush with national media fame but not its last. The intersection was featured in a segment on Joan Lunden's *Good Morning, America* program in 1987.

By the time Duany made it to town, there were already plans in motion to add a traffic signal at Confusion Corner to make the intersection less

Dedication of Martin County Hospital. *Martin County Historical Society.*

confusing. The Stuart City Commission had decided in December 1987 to go along with the state Department of Transportation's plans to turn Confusion Corner into a conventional intersection with a traffic signal. That change was part of the state's plans for the new Roosevelt Bridge, which was then expected to have its southern terminus nearby.

"Fixing" Confusion Corner was expected to cost about $1.3 million, which state officials offered to pay. "Confusion Corner may be historic, but it's history," read the opening line of a December 31, 1987 article in the *Palm Beach Post*. The DOT plan also would have involved closing the stretch of Old Dixie Highway at Confusion Corner, which would have had a profound impact on traffic, too.

Joan Jefferson said the state's offer to pay for the improvements made sense, especially since local roads were becoming increasingly more crowded. Duany pushed back against that idea, though. He said tampering with Confusion Corner would take away one of the community's unique assets.

There continued to be hearings about DOT's plans for the intersection, in which self-identified "sentimentalists" fought for the status quo. Duany sided with the sentimentalists. "This is probably the best-known postcard of Stuart," Duany said of Confusion Corner in the August 24, 1988 edition of the *Stuart News*. "To destroy that bit of intensity would be a tragedy."

DOT officials eventually relented.

According to the September 28, 1988 minutes from the Main Street board of directors' meeting, DOT told local officials the agency was "wiping its hands" of Confusion Corner. Following one of the public hearings, DOT officials announced that they were postponing any changes at Confusion

Woman crossing railroad tracks in downtown Stuart, 1905. *Martin County Library System.*

Corner for at least five years, according to a report in the November 23, 1988 edition of the *Palm Beach Post.*

Then in November 1988, state transportation officials said plans for the alignment of the new Roosevelt Bridge made overhauling Confusion Corner unnecessary.

Residents never seemed very interested in the traffic signal plans, anyway. Through the years, they had learned to embrace the intersection's quirkiness. Some nearby businesses even used it as part of their marketing efforts. For example, at one time, there was a business near the intersection called Confusion Records. The Florida Insurance Center, located a short walking distance away, noted how convenient its location was for unlucky motorists who might need to file accident claims.

Still, in talking to some local residents, Confusion Corner's reputation as a magnet for fender benders seems largely overblown. "I never once saw an accident at Confusion Corner," said Nancy Smith, even though the *Stuart News* office overlooked the intersection. For the most part, Smith said locals approach the intersection with the appropriate amount of caution to avoid trouble.

Thomas Weber said the current configuration, with a landscaped median at the roundabout's center, is actually an improvement over the way Confusion Corner used to be in the 1970s and 1980s. "Back in those days, it was more difficult, by quite a bit," Weber said. "They put a lot of effort in the way it is now. It seems it's still not an easy intersection to travel through, but it's way better than it was, especially with so much more traffic in there."

Although its reputation as a traffic hazard might be slightly exaggerated, Confusion Corner survived the 1980s intact. It was, and still is, one of the unique features that gives Stuart its charm.

Chapter 13

NEW URBAN GURU'S WATER TOWER IDEA GETS DOUSED

A s mentioned in previous chapters, Stuart residents and city officials greeted most of Andrés Duany's ideas with great enthusiasm. After all, he was considered to be one of the leading figures in the urban planning industry. He may not have truly been a "messiah," as one of his detractors had mockingly called him, but his suggestions did carry great weight.

Which isn't to say that there weren't some areas where the locals pushed back. In some cases, they decided to chart their own course.

Duany's suggestion about painting the water tower was a perfect example. It came about three years after his initial set of recommendations, which had been received with much appreciation and acclaim.

According to the Historical Marker Database, the water tower was originally constructed in 1959. The image of an American flag was added to its design at the suggestion of Martin County High School's class of 1976, as a way of commemorating the nation's bicentennial anniversary.

When Duany arrived in town to talk about the water tower fifteen years later, the bicentennial was a distant memory. Duany thought it was important to keep the water tower in good condition. With Martin County limiting building heights to four stories, the tower was one of the most visible features on the downtown skyline.

He favored keeping the city's name on the water tower, in lettering "as large as possible." Yet Duany thought the patriotic paint scheme was a bit much. His preference was for cloth flags on flagpoles, not giant murals. He also recommended painting the tower a color that was like the colors other cities were using on their water towers.

It was a political miscalculation on his part.

"The city was totally unprepared for the furor this would engender," according to the Main Street board's minutes. "The Gulf War was in full operation, and the citizens were outraged that we would remove the faded pop-art flag and replace it with a monotone green color."

Duany actually called his recommended paint scheme "pearl grey," but others insisted it was, in fact, green. "I wish they wouldn't call it 'pea green,'" Duany lamented at one point during what became a protracted debate about the tower's color scheme.

The *Stuart News* balked at Duany's choice. In an editorial, the newspaper denounced it as "too sickly a hue."

Sally Swartz, the *Palm Beach Post* columnist, also had a few thoughts on the subject. "How about a bright, hot, neon pink?" Swartz suggested, more than likely with tongue firmly planted in cheek.

Journalists were hardly the only ones with concerns. Opponents of the revamped paint scheme included the local chapters of the Boy Scouts and the Veterans of Foreign Wars, the Main Street group, assorted military servicemembers and other citizens.

It wasn't just the choice of colors that bothered the dissenters. Many saw removing the flag imagery as unpatriotic.

Mabel Witham was one of the most outspoken protestors. A Detroit native, she was a special needs teacher who married into one of the community's pioneering families. Witham Field, the local airport, was named in honor of her brother-in-law, Homer Witham, a navy pilot who was killed during World War II.

To draw attention to her concerns, Mabel Witham wrapped herself in the flag that had covered Homer Witham's coffin when she was speaking before the Stuart City Commission about the water tower. She was backed by a chorus of veterans who said it would be unpatriotic to remove the flag art.

"After several meetings, and a hearty debate, a 3–2 vote was taken to paint the water tower with the flag and the name of the city," the Main Street board meeting minutes read.

In the overall scheme of things, it wasn't a huge setback for Duany or his ideas. The city did keep the tower intact, with the name clearly visible, as Duany had suggested.

There were other deviations from his grand plans as well. Downtown Stuart does have a post office branch, although it's located a few blocks away

Water tower, circa 1926. *Martin County Library System.*

from the historic district. There's no library downtown, either. The nearest one is located near the intersection of Monterey Road and East Ocean Boulevard, well outside of downtown.

While Duany encouraged live/work spaces, with first-floor businesses topped by apartments or condominiums on upper floors, that design concept never really caught on in downtown Stuart.

A lot of his recommendations were adopted, however, including one to resist the state Department of Transportation's efforts to route the new Roosevelt Bridge through an area that would have essentially wiped out a major chunk of the historic district.

Had locals not listened to Duany about some of the larger items on his checklist, downtown Stuart wouldn't exist as we know it today.

Chapter 14

A BRIDGE TOO NEAR

C onfusion Corner wasn't the only Stuart traffic nuisance that was immortalized on bumper stickers. What's now known as the "old" Roosevelt Bridge also had that distinction, minus the loveable charm locals associated with Confusion Corner.

The bridge on Old Dixie Highway, also known as A1A, connected the northern part of the city with downtown at a relatively narrow spot in the St. Lucie River. Construction of the first span began in 1932, with a budget of $500,000. The bridge was dedicated on January 9, 1934, according to TCPalm stories about the bridge's history. A full thirty years later, in 1964, a second span was added to the bridge, at a cost of $4 million.

Those two spans, with drawbridges, served as the main entrance and exit points for downtown Stuart for decades. By the 1980s, if not before, they were showing their age. The drawbridges sometimes malfunctioned, causing traffic backups on either side of the river. Even when they were working properly, the drawbridges had to be raised frequently to allow boats to pass underneath.

The mouth of the St. Lucie River anchors one end of a canal system that extends to Lake Okeechobee and, beyond that, the Gulf of Mexico. That meant the canal system was the boating equivalent of a major interstate highway. Having the bridge raised for extended periods of time caused traffic backups into the heart of downtown—which locals embraced with their typical wry sense of humor. The local Police Explorer Post printed bumper stickers with the slogan "I was stuck on the Roosevelt Bridge."

Stuart residents may have been good-natured about the occasional tie-ups around Confusion Corner, but they were less tolerant of delays at the bridge.

By the 1980s, the Florida Department of Transportation was working on plans for a replacement bridge. To some, those plans didn't seem like much of an improvement.

In an October 31, 2007 TCPalm article looking back on the new bridge's construction, Joan Jefferson described the different ideas DOT officials had as "a marvelous compromise from six alternate plans, none good. They wanted to build eight lanes of traffic and tear down most of the town."

DOT officials had narrowed those six options down to four by 1987. According to a *Palm Beach Post* article from February 8 of that year, the least destructive of those options would have required thirty-nine businesses and four homes to be demolished. Rather than follow the path of Old Dixie Highway as the old bridge did, the new bridge was planned for US 1, with the total number of lanes expanding from four to six. The worst-case scenario would have required the removal of sixty-six businesses and eleven homes.

"It sounds like they're wiping out half of downtown Stuart," developer Randy Haisfield complained in one *Post* article.

Stuart bridges, 1920. *Martin County Library System.*

None of the options was particularly cheap, either. The projected costs ranged from $62.2 million to $82.4 million.

In December 1987, Stuart and Martin County officials were publicly expressing their concerns about DOT's plans, which would have converted Confusion Corner into a regular four-way intersection and destroyed some downtown businesses, including the old Dyer's Department Store building. As an alternative, city and county officials wanted a six-lane bridge, roughly fifty-five feet high, just west of the old bridge's location. That would have kept the southern end of the new bridge from wiping out much of the historic downtown area.

By the following year, DOT was looking at other options, including moving the bridge so far east it would bypass the historic district entirely.

Andrés Duany arrived in Stuart in 1988 and jumped into the middle of the fray. It was clear from many of his statements and written comments that he held the DOT in very low regard. During one of his planning meetings, he got into a confrontation with DOT officials who said it was too late in the process to consider major deviations from the previously discussed alternatives for the new bridge's construction. Duany assured them, in no uncertain terms, that it was not too late.

As previously noted, Duany had accused DOT of destroying more American cities than General Sherman had during his Civil War march through Georgia. Rather than allowing the state to dictate the terms of how the bridge would be built, Duany recommended the city "control the Department of Transportation."

He was willing to concede a new bridge might be "inevitable and possibly necessary," but he wasn't willing to sacrifice both spans of the old bridge in the process. He argued that it was important to keep at least one of them as a gateway into downtown. He suggested there would be dire consequences if both spans were demolished. "Their removal will turn the downtown commercial streets into a huge cul-de-sac devoid of through traffic," he said.

In addition to keeping one of the old bridge spans, Duany thought the new bridge should have six lanes instead of eight. With some of the downtown traffic still using the old bridge, he figured that would be enough to adequately manage traffic flow while saving as many buildings as possible.

Duany's words weren't the last ones on the subject. Discussions about various bridge designs and alignments continued throughout the decade and into the 1990s.

A group called the Save Our Stuart Task Force was formed to represent citizens concerned about the direction the bridge plans were taking. Avron

Rifkin, the task force's co-chairman, summed up some of the group's frustrations in an April 26, 1989 article in the *Palm Beach Post*: "After this bridge has caused the ruination of Stuart, where do we take our bucket of tears?"

The task force suggested alternatives to DOT's bridge design, including a tunnel or aqueduct beneath the river. Supporters of those alternatives estimated the cost of a tunnel or aqueduct at $49 million, less than half the $100 million DOT was projecting for the new bridge's cost.

DOT officials disputed the cost estimates for a tunnel, saying the true expense would be much higher than task force members thought. Also, DOT said shifting from a bridge to a tunnel would require a new round of environmental impact studies, which could delay the project for years.

In a March 3, 1989 editorial, the *Stuart News* seemed to be in agreement with the DOT, suggesting it was too late in the process to return to the drawing board.

In a guest column in the *Palm Beach Post* later that year, Joan Jefferson essentially made the same argument. She urged the community to stay the course, citing the potential loss of financing if the project had to endure extensive delays.

The Save Our Stuart group came up with another alternative, a forty-five-foot-high drawbridge, but again the DOT rejected that idea as being impractical to build.

The group picked up an ally in City Commissioner Charles Foster, who liked the drawbridge proposal. He and Jefferson became political rivals on that and a few other issues, which was unusual on the Stuart City Commission at the time.

Jeffrey Krauskopf, who also served on the commission during those years, said a lot of the positive changes that occurred downtown in the 1980s and early 1990s were made possible because of the lack of political discord. "We were five horses pulling the wagon in the same direction," Krauskopf said of the commission. "It was just esprit de corps back then."

For the most part, that was true. However, Krauskopf noted that Foster wasn't shy about taking contrarian views from time to time. "He enjoyed playing the devil's advocate, which was good for us," Krauskopf said.

Jefferson wanted to steer clear of the task force's more radical ideas, including the tunnel or a new drawbridge. DOT wanted a bridge with a higher span to avoid the drawbridge problems the old Roosevelt Bridge had experienced. In an August 26, 1989 letter to the editor in the *Stuart News*, Save Our Stuart called the high spans DOT envisioned "a gross overdesign."

Downtown Stuart, 1920. *Martin County Library System.*

There were other issues residents had, besides the new bridge's proposed height. At a 1990 public hearing, some expressed concern that the large structure would divide the city. Others worried the new bridge would become a magnet for homeless people, providing shelter from the heat and rain. Others thought the new bridge could hurt boating and bring more car traffic to Stuart.

Ultimately, though, the commission voted to support a sixty-five-foot-high bridge, while preserving one of the old bridge's two spans. Although many other options had been considered and rejected, the proposal the commission approved, with Foster dissenting, was similar to what Duany had recommended a couple of years earlier.

Construction work on the new bridge, also called the Roosevelt Bridge, began in 1992 and was completed in 1997 at a cost of $83.7 million.

The aesthetic appeal of the new spans, which tower above the rest of the skyline, is a matter for debate. But by routing the bridge along US 1, west of downtown's core, most of the city's historic buildings were saved. For residents tired of the frequent traffic tie-ups associated with the old bridge, the replacement product was good enough.

Chapter 15

"A LONG AND TEDIOUS VOYAGE" IN SEARCH OF DOWNTOWN MARINA

The new Roosevelt Bridge wasn't the only project that remained under discussion for many years during the 1980s and 1990s. There was also talk about building a new marina downtown. Actually, some city officials had been dreaming about a downtown marina for decades. In the 1970s, putting a marina at Shepard Park had been under consideration, but the plans fizzled out.

During the 1980s, the idea of putting a marina somewhere downtown seemed to be gaining some political traction again. A task force was formed to study the issue. After completing its work, the group concluded an eighty-eight-slip marina located on the waterfront behind Stuart City Hall was "environmentally, physically and fiscally feasible," Joan Jefferson wrote in a letter to the Community Redevelopment Agency in October 1986.

There were some concerns raised by the state agencies consulted by the task force, though. Protecting manatees, slow-moving sea mammals frequently killed or injured by motorboats, was near the top of the list of worries. Providing a place for boats to dock downtown could imperil manatees in the area. To lower the risk for manatees, Jefferson proposed slow speed limits for boats traveling in that area.

That wasn't the only potential obstacle to a marina's construction. Some people worried a marina would attract houseboats with "live-aboard" residents, who might be inclined to dump their sewage tanks directly into the river. Even without the marina, city officials had been fielding complaints about northerners who docked and emptied their waste at other spots along the shoreline.

Another concern was that boats in the marina would be prone to fuel spills that also would pollute the river.

There were also questions about how much dredging would be required to complete a marina, as well as the potential impact of extra boat traffic on navigational channels.

In a 1986 *Stuart News* article, Jefferson said it could take up to two years to get the necessary permits required for marina construction.

A *Stuart News* editorial warned planning for a marina would be "a long and tedious voyage through a bureaucratic sea."

Despite that warning, city commissioners continued to explore the idea. "The marina will be the catalyst to downtown revitalization," Commissioner Charles Foster said in the December 28, 1986 issue of the *Stuart News*. "It will bring a new dimension to downtown. I believe the marina is almost a necessity."

There was a preferred site, located behind the Stuart Feed Store, the Stuart Recreation Center and Huckleberry's Restaurant.

Developers were invited to submit proposals for the project, which was expected to cost about $25 million. Four proposals were submitted to the city, including an ambitious one that called for a ninety-slip marina, a one-hundred-room hotel, a Charley's Crab restaurant, a plaza of shops and boutiques and a three-story garage. "I think the future of downtown is

Downtown business district, 1955. *Martin County Library System.*

bright," James W. Hall, the developer who made that proposal, said in a February 17, 1987 *Stuart News* article.

Another proposal called for the feed store, one of the city's oldest buildings, to be converted into a restaurant to complement the marina development.

A couple of the proposals called for more boat slips than Hall's plan included. However, city commissioners selected Hall's plan as their preferred option.

The plans didn't have the entire community's unqualified support. By April 1987, about seventy people had signed a petition opposing the marina project, which they feared would block the waterfront views of residents at the community center. "The people [at the center] object because of the beautiful view," Jensen Beach resident Joseph Forsberg said in the April 11, 1987 issue of the *Stuart News*. "The waterfront is becoming less and less."

The city's leaders were thinking about building a new recreation center at a different location, freeing up space for a marina, but that wasn't the type of solution some residents wanted.

The Department of Transportation's plans for the new Roosevelt Bridge also complicated planning for a marina. At that time, state officials were looking at a path for the new bridge that would have cut across land proposed for the marina and hotel.

Then there was the issue of getting the marina approved by various state and federal agencies. To streamline the process, Jefferson suggested having all the agencies involved in permitting get together for a summit on the project, as opposed to having each of them work independently on their own review processes. A *Palm Beach Post* editorial praised Jefferson for her attempt to make navigating the bureaucratic seas a little less treacherous.

In January 1988, Jefferson received letters from U.S. Senators Lawton Chiles and Bob Graham, Governor Bob Martinez and Congressman Tom Lewis, lending their political support to the marina.

Although Jefferson was successful in arranging a one-day summit involving the different regulatory agencies, new obstacles kept cropping up. The Martin County Conservation Alliance opposed the project because it wanted the rec center to remain a public facility, rather than having that property used for private development. A group called Concerned Boaters said the proposed site was unsuitable.

To help with the planning process, city leaders sent a delegation to Miami's Bayside Market to get ideas about marina development.

By 1990, the state had granted its required approvals for the project, but the permit it issued was due to expire by 1993. A recession and continued

Stuart Feed Store customers, circa 1945. *Martin County Library System.*

discussions about the new Roosevelt Bridge's location continued to hinder the process.

In March 1992, city commissioners again opened the process for developers to submit proposals. One of the responses to the city's request called for a 119-slip marina, a convention center, improvements to the recreation center and parking. A hotel was no longer part of those plans.

More than two years later, in July 1994, the commission approved plans for a 115-slip marina, a 24-unit rental complex, a 150-seat restaurant, a renovated recreation center and a redesigned Flagler Avenue.

The commission selected Florida Marina Management Corp. to develop the project. It never happened. The company the city had selected was already having financial difficulties related to its work on the Fort Pierce Yachting

Center, a mixed-use project with some of the same land-use components as had been envisioned for the Stuart marina complex. Although the company did some of the planning work on the Stuart marina, its president, Audie Lee Morris, died of cancer on July 3, 1995. His death threw the project further behind schedule.

When it became apparent Florida Marine Management Corp. would not be able to honor its commitments to complete the Stuart project, other developers expressed interest in taking over.

However, the same public concerns that had dogged the project for years remained. People still worried about the amount of dredging that might be required and how it could affect navigation channels. Also, the rec center patrons continued to express concerns about losing their waterfront view. Unlike many of the other items on the city's wish list for downtown revitalization, the marina project ran into too many political and logistical difficulties to overcome.

In 2001, the Southpoint Anchorage opened on the southwest side of the Roosevelt Bridge, a different site than the one that had been under discussion during the 1980s and 1990s. Eight years later, Sunset Bay Marina and Anchorage opened at that same site.

Downtown eventually got its marina, but it wasn't part of the sweeping changes that were happening in the latter part of the twentieth century.

Chapter 16

ICONIC DOWNTOWN BUILDINGS AFFECTED BY REDEVELOPMENT

t didn't happen, but those plans for a downtown marina could have affected the city's oldest building, the Stuart Feed Store. The two-story clapboard building, which looks a bit like one of those shops shown along dusty streets in old Western movies, opened in 1901 as the George W. Parks General Merchandise Store. For decades, it was an important community gathering spot and supplied a wide range of goods to generations of customers. The store was relocated more than once during its history before settling into its permanent address at 101 Flagler Avenue near city hall.

It endured natural disasters, including hurricanes, as well as changes in ownership through the years. The store's name also went through some changes, from Stuart Mercantile to Stuart Feed Supply to Stuart Feed Store.

The February 4, 1981 issue of the *Stuart News* included a lengthy feature story explaining how the store managed to survive through the ups and downs of many business cycles, including the then-recent surge in popularity of malls and shopping centers. "Folksy charm of Stuart Feed Supply keeps 'em coming back for generations," the headline on the story read. "It has been written up almost as many times, and in as many places, as the Taj Mahal," the article said. "It's the kind of place you have to see to believe."

As the name suggested, the store did sell feed, but that was only a portion of its inventory. The store carried a vast assortment of home and outdoor supplies, the equivalent of a Lowe's or Home Depot store in the decades before chain stores dominated the retailing industry.

Like other longstanding businesses in the downtown area, Stuart Feed Store was known for its personalized service that led to many repeat customers. The store didn't take credit cards but would accept personal checks, because Alice Borello, president of the company that then owned the store, said, "We believe in the honesty of people and we haven't been disappointed."

By late 1986, the city was planning the downtown marina on property that included the store site. There were discussions about moving the old building to the nearby recreation center property and possibly converting it into a seafood restaurant.

The Borellos had offered the building for sale but were unable to come to terms with city leaders on a deal. Apparently, though, the Borello family had a change of heart sometime between December 1986 and late February 1987.

According to a February 23, 1987 *Stuart News* article, Anthony Borello professed to be excited about plans to build a downtown marina where the store was sitting. "I think it's terrific," he said. "It'll be good for the city."

At that point, the family had operated the store for about twenty years. The Borellos had rejected an offer from New Jersey marina developer Lon Gatti because they didn't like the terms of the deal, either.

At the time, the city was considering several proposals from developers for a marina. Some involved relocating the building to a different site. Others would have kept it in place but changed its use to a ship store or a restaurant.

The Borellos made an offer to sell the property to the city, but that offer was refused.

As we know from the previous chapter, plans for a downtown marina never came together during the 1980s, so the Stuart Feed Store remained where it was. The city did eventually purchase the store, along with two adjoining lots, for $385,000 in 1988.

The next year, city officials were planning a different type of adaptive reuse for the building. Encouraged by their success in obtaining a grant to renovate the old courthouse (which will be discussed in an upcoming chapter), city leaders were hoping to get another grant from the Florida Department of State to renovate the building.

Peter Jefferson, Joan's husband and the lead architect for the restoration project, estimated about $130,000 would be needed to cover the expected costs. The renovation plans included a number of structural repairs, as well as the addition of a thirty-seat theater. "We want to use it as a museum and an exhibition place to show off old Stuart," City Commissioner

Joan Jefferson was quoted as saying in the September 9, 1989 issue of the *Stuart News*.

Among the ideas under consideration was selling replicas of the goods sold during the store's early years to help cover the cost of the building's maintenance and upkeep.

The city got the grant funding needed to refurbish the building and then later turned over responsibility for its operations to Stuart Heritage, a group founded in 1988 to focus on preserving Martin County history. The Stuart Feed Store became the Stuart Heritage Museum, which remains open in the present day. As the "new" name suggests, the museum contains artifacts showcasing local history.

The store wasn't the only old downtown building to see significant changes during the 1980s. The Stuart Department Store, located at 141 Southwest Flagler Avenue, only a short distance from the Stuart Feed Store, also saw profound changes during the 1980s. Much like the Stuart Feed Store, the Stuart Department Store was for decades a constant in a sea of change downtown. The Kanarek family had purchased the store in 1938 and operated it as a family-run business from that point forward.

The September 29, 1982 edition of the *Stuart News* carried a lengthy feature story on the store, which was then in its forty-fourth year of operation. The store had been in the same location for twenty-eight years at that point. The store was owned by the Kanarek and Auerbach families, who, according to the article, "have succeeded in good times and bad without help from anyone except a very loyal band of customers."

The Stuart Department Store wasn't known for its frills or marketing gimmicks. Rather, the store won a loyal following by providing brand-name merchandise and personalized service. It wasn't uncommon for the store's sales staff to greet customers by name. The *Stuart News* article recounted cases of customers from out of state ordering merchandise from Stuart Department Store because they had built strong relationships with the staff there.

Unfortunately, that didn't last.

In its November 28, 1984 issue, the *Stuart News* reported the owners were planning to close up shop on January 5 of the following year. The family members who were running the store at the time were battling age and various health issues. The younger generation had decided to pursue other interests outside the family business.

Selling to different owners wasn't considered a viable option. "We are proud of the name we've established over the years," co-owner Max

Auerbach said. "That's why we didn't want to sell that name to someone who might not live up to that reputation."

The family wasn't interested in relocating to a storefront at Treasure Coast Mall, located a few miles away in Jensen Beach.

Auerbach said he had received "the phone calls and tears" since the planned closure was announced to staff and customers.

The store didn't make it until its planned closure date, though. The December 18, 1984 issue of the *Stuart News* noted the store had closed a few weeks early because it had sold all of the goods it was trying to liquidate.

Only a few months later, the building had a new owner. The Stuart City Commission voted unanimously to buy the building from owners Max Auerbach and Irving Kanarek, according to the April 23, 1985 issue of the *Stuart News*. The commission agreed to pay $400,000—a price that was $32,000 above the property's appraised value. Commissioners said the 6,200-square-foot, Art Deco–style building could come in handy if city hall, located next door, needed to expand at some point in the future.

Until then, city officials were planning to lease the building to other tenants. Some of the prospects at the time included the Martin County Water Department, the Martin County Office of Veterans Affairs and Senator Tom Lewis.

At the time, the city's leaders were very mindful of the potential to revitalize historic buildings and put them to productive use. At the same meeting where the commissioners agreed to buy the Stuart Department Store, they also created a nine-member Downtown Redevelopment Ad Hoc Committee charged with overseeing revitalization efforts.

It took the city a couple of years to find a suitable tenant to take over the building, but it happened. A story in the June 3, 1987 issue of the *Stuart News* covered the grand opening of the new offices for Keith and Schnars, an engineering, planning and surveying firm. The firm was leasing the building from the city and expected to spend somewhere between $70,000 and $100,000 on renovations.

Garth Horne, the firm's regional manager, said the business wanted a location next to city hall because that was "where the action is." "We have a keen interest in the redevelopment of the downtown area, so we are pleased to be part of that," Horne told the newspaper. "The building is also one of the best ones we could find that is big enough to hold all our employees, and all our plans for the future. More than that, though, it's just a neat place."

Greene's Department Store, one of Stuart Department Store's competitors, also went through some changes during the 1980s. Greene's Department

Store was founded in February 1924 and had operated at the same downtown location, 215 Southwest Flagler, since 1941. Robert Greene, the son of the store's founder, had been running operations since 1952. According to a November 19, 1985 *Stuart News* article, Greene's was "probably" the city's oldest family-run department store.

However, after searching for someone to take over the business, Greene decided to shut it down. "I'm really sorry about this," Greene told the newspaper. "But I'm 57 years old and I've got other things I want to do, and, you know, if I went another 10 years, I'd be 67."

Greene landed on his feet. By April of the following year, he was renovating the building's upper floor so it could be leased as office space. The Pipette, a children's clothing store owned by Julie Preast, was already occupying the ground floor.

"Old is in," an article in the April 9, 1986 issue of the *Stuart News* said. "And you need only look at the changing face of downtown Stuart to realize that a number of property owners have their minds rooted firmly in the past. Greene is just the latest to discover what's old is new again."

Preast said she opened the Pipette because she sensed downtown's resurgence was about to take off. "I felt there was so much potential there," she said in an interview decades later.

The Holleran Building, located near the Greene's Department Store site at 219 Flagler, was also part of the 1980s trend of revitalizing and reusing older buildings. It was undergoing a $400,000 renovation that began in July 1985.

Yet another of downtown's grand old buildings to be swept up in the wave of change was the Pelican Hotel. Governor John Martin, for whom Martin County is named, was a silent partner in the hotel's ownership

Women's Club library, 1920. *Martin County Library System.*

Stuart school, 1912. *Martin County Library System.*

group during its early years. Work on the hotel, originally called the Dixie Pelican, began in 1925, with a construction budget of $170,000. The three-story building on Osceola Street overlooking the St. Lucie River became a favorite place for the rich and famous to stay while visiting Stuart.

Members of the production crew filming *Little Laura and Big John*, a movie about the notorious Ashley Gang that roamed through the region during the Great Depression era, were among the many VIPs who stayed at the Pelican.

However, a murder-suicide at the hotel cast a pall over its reputation and led to its decline.

Among the many people who worked at the Pelican Hotel through the years was a young dishwasher named Willie Gary, who picked up extra money at that job while attending high school. Gary became a highly successful and flamboyant attorney, known for his ability to win large judgments against large corporations. He became so successful that he was portrayed by actor Jamie Foxx in the 2023 movie *The Burial*, which focused on one of those high-profile cases he handled.

During the 1980s, Gary decided to buy the Pelican Hotel, his former workplace, and turn it into his new workplace. He reportedly spent $3 million converting the hotel into his law offices, which he renamed Waterside Place.

At the time he bought the building, there were two men still working at the Pelican who were there during Gary's busboy days. One had treated

Gary with kindness, while the other one had been mean and used racial slurs in Gary's presence. Gary kept the nicer man on his staff, while firing the meaner one in a bit of karmic justice.

It wasn't only buildings housing private businesses that underwent transformations. Remember the old courthouse building, left intact when county officials had made arrangements for a new courthouse, jail and government offices during the 1980s?

Well, it wasn't left to sit idle, either.

Chapter 17

"UGLY" ART DECO BUILDING BECOMES AN ARTISTS' SHRINE

I f readers will recall from chapter 5, Stuart and Martin County residents had a spirited debate about where a new courthouse needed to be built. Downtown advocates worried building the new courthouse outside of the central city area would be a death blow for a neighborhood that was already in decline.

In the mid-1980s, however, the chamber of commerce was advocating for the courthouse's relocation to free up more space for parking downtown.

In a February 14, 1985 letter to the editor published in the *Stuart News*, Joan Jefferson had argued such a move could be ruinous for downtown. "Who will support the restaurants and businesses that opened close to the existing courthouse and administration facilities to provide necessary services?" she wrote. "Will they have to move to stay in business? More unoccupied space?"

In another letter to the newspaper a month and a day later, local resident Frederick E. Neumeyer countered by suggesting that Stuart's fate was already sealed and that de-incorporating the city might be a viable option. "Maybe Stuart is dying," Neumeyer wrote. "Does Stuart really exist today as the social and economic center of Martin County?"

In the end, of course, after a couple of years of discussing various scenarios, county officials agreed to build the new courthouse next to the old one. But that left open the question of what to do with the old courthouse after the new one was built.

The old courthouse had a storied past. Chalker & Lund, a West Palm Beach construction company, won the contract to construct the building for

$24,650 in 1937. The project was funded by the federal Works Progress Administration as part of President Franklin D. Roosevelt's New Deal.

The two-story building at 80 East Ocean Boulevard was the first structure in the county constructed specifically to serve as a courthouse. Prior to its construction, justice was meted out from buildings that were originally used for other purposes. For example, the old courthouse's predecessor was a building constructed in 1908 to serve as a schoolhouse in what was then the Dade County town of Potsdam.

However, once the new courthouse was built, some in the community were ready to give the old courthouse the death sentence. In a November 16, 1988 letter to the editor published in the *Stuart News*, local resident Mildred Marsteller complained the old courthouse was blocking the view of the new building. Marsteller described the old courthouse as "an old, antiquated courthouse with no unique architectural design, hindering and distracting the view of this lovely new building."

She was hardly the only one who felt that way. While the old building's Art Deco architecture was becoming popular again, there were others in the community who thought it was a poor example of the style.

Nevertheless, in December 1988, the *Stuart News* reported that work was scheduled to begin the following March to remove asbestos from the building and demolish two wings and an annex that had been added to the original structure. By June of the next year, city officials had convinced the state legislature to provide $200,000 to renovate the old courthouse, using a grant from the Florida Department of State.

That didn't quiet the critics. In another *Stuart News* letter to the editor, published April 25, 1989, local residents Gene and Elizabeth Landsdown argued the old courthouse wasn't worth saving. "I will not vote for any commissioner or for restoring downtown Stuart," they wrote.

Peter Jefferson, Joan Jefferson's husband, was selected to serve as the renovation project's lead architect, according to a June 26, 1989 article in the *Stuart News*.

Philip Braden, another local architect who was one of the building's critics, predicted the renovation project would face cost overruns. "That will be the beginning of it, but not the end of it," Braden said of the project's budget.

Braden considered the renovation work a waste of taxpayer money because he didn't think the building was worth saving in the first place. "It's still pretty ugly," Braden said. "It should have been torn down."

Circuit Court judge Marc Cianca agreed with Braden that there were better uses for the money. "I don't see why they didn't level the doggone thing," Cianca said.

The judge also urged city officials to consider how the building was going to be used after the renovation work was finished. He suggested the building might see new life as a library. "If you're going to keep it and put a lot of money into it, it needs to be something more than a shrine," Cianca said.

Braden did offer a bit of tongue-in-cheek praise for the decision to remove the building's wings, which had been added to the original structure in the 1950s. "The less of it that shows, the better I'll like it," Braden said.

Peter Jefferson took issue with Braden's and Cianca's assertions, saying there was no need to get rid of the old building.

In a November 7, 1989 editorial, the *Stuart News* came down on the side of Jefferson and other preservation advocates in the city. The newspaper's editorial board suggested both the old and new courthouse could coexist, like the old and new state capitol buildings in Tallahassee. "There is room in Stuart for both old and new courthouses," the editorial read. "We hope the restoration project moves rapidly, and that the other downtown work fulfills the high hopes of officials and local residents."

While the debate continued back and forth, the renovation work was finished. The July 4, 1990 edition of the *Stuart News* included a story about the dedication ceremony for the newly renovated building. "While not as

Osceola Street, circa 1942. *Martin County Library System.*

flamboyant as the Miami Beach Art Deco buildings, the old Martin County Courthouse had a dignified touch of style—one befitting a government building," the story said. "Once again, the Art Deco section of the old Martin County Courthouse is pleasing the community."

Peter Jefferson expressed satisfaction with the way the building looked, post-renovation. "It turned out to be an even more beautiful and handsome building than I thought it would be," he said. "It's a richly detailed and high quality building that no one could afford to build today."

In 1991, the county began leasing the building to the local arts council for use as an arts and cultural center. It is still used for that purpose at the time of this writing.

Both the old and new courthouses were considered important elements of downtown Stuart's rebirth. Peter and Joan Jefferson both played major roles in the decisions that kept them anchoring downtown. The old courthouse renovations weren't the project most closely associated with the Jeffersons, though. Both husband and wife were involved in restoring an iconic building that some considered to be the turning point in the process of bringing downtown back to life.

Chapter 18

JEFFERSONS "PUT THEIR MONEY WHERE THEIR MOUTHS WERE"

A s previous chapters have suggested, downtown Stuart's rebirth didn't occur overnight. And there was no single event that transformed what had been a somewhat blighted area into a showplace enjoyed by locals and visitors from around the world.

Certainly, there were a number of key moments along the way. Getting residents to volunteer for the first Community Service Day foreshadowed the community's can-do spirit. Convincing the Martin County Commission not to move the main courthouse out of downtown saved many businesses from financial disaster. The Dancin' in the Streets events brought the community together and helped raise money to aid the revitalization efforts. Restoring the Lyric Theatre provided a cultural center for downtown and also demonstrated the value of putting older buildings back into use. Implementing Andrés Duany's master plan, with its many different components, was a critical step in the process. However, the story that some residents and business owners who were around during the 1980s and 1990s seem to remember as the turning point dealt with the Post Office Arcade.

Construction on the building at 252 West Osceola Street was completed in 1925, according to an article written by Alice and Greg Luckhardt for TCPalm, an online newspaper. According to the Luckhardts' article, published on October 2, 2012, the concrete-and-stucco building was designed to accommodate not only the post office but also ten other stores in an arcade connecting Osceola and Seminole.

Architect Gerald J. O'Reilly designed the building, which was financed by Edward A. Fuge, president of the Bank of Stuart and the Southland

Bond & Mortgage Company. It was built by contractor Sam Matthews at a cost of $50,000.

The post office served as the building's anchor tenant until the late 1950s, when a new branch location opened a few blocks away. Losing the post office wasn't the death knell for the arcade building, though. There were other businesses that continued to operate there for decades. At one point, a Piggly Wiggly grocery store was located there. Later, Florida Power & Light had one of its regional offices there. However, by the 1980s, Florida Power & Light and most of the other tenants had moved out.

Julie Preast, one of the downtown shop owners during the 1980s, remembers the loss of the utility company's workers as a big economic blow.

"When Florida Power & Light decided to move away, there were fewer professionals doing anything downtown because they [FPL] had a large group of employees," Preast recalled decades later. "It truly affected business, losing the Florida Power & Light offices. It really hurt downtown dramatically."

The arcade building itself started to decline after the utility company's departure, too. "When FPL left, there was pretty much nothing in there," recalled Jim Dirks, another downtown shop owner. "A lot of homeless people started living in there. The building was in disrepair. The roof was leaking. I remember there was some broken glass in there."

Nancy Smith, the former *Stuart News* editor, said the Post Office Arcade's decline was a bleak symbol of the ragged state of downtown during those years. "It was down at the heels," Smith said. "Some people thought it should just be razed and the whole downtown should go. And build condos or waterfront housing. People didn't want the downtown in Stuart, Florida, to be US 1. That was what they felt their option was."

Despite its condition, the building was about to get a couple of new tenants: Peter and Joan Jefferson.

For more than two decades, the couple had been living in a beautiful riverfront home overlooking the St. Lucie River that, at one time, had only been accessible by water. The home was built in 1908 and then thoroughly restored by Peter Jefferson after the couple took ownership of the home.

An article in the October 2, 1988 edition of the *Stuart News* described the home as an architectural marvel, filled with eccentric touches that reflected the Jeffersons' unique personalities. "Concentrated in details, the home exudes warmth," the article in the newspaper's "Home Show" section read. "There is virtually no awareness of paint, paper or fabric. No pattern or color scheme to bind up the total effect. But there are warm hues of wood and natural materials providing the perfect background for their collection of artfully placed compositions."

The personal touches included an abstract sculpture of a large leopard on the front porch, an antique wheelchair at the head of the dining room table and a Mexican skeleton candelabra in the hallway. There was special meaning attached to some of the décor. For example, Peter Jefferson explained the antique wheelchair this way. "It's a projection of things to come for all of us, so we made it an affectionate piece of furniture," he told the newspaper.

As beautiful as their home was, the Jeffersons were destined to sell it so they could pursue a project that was critical in reshaping the face of downtown Stuart.

In an October 5, 1989 column in the *Palm Beach Post*, Sally Swartz described a "change of life" sale the Jeffersons held in which they auctioned off 75 percent of their possessions in preparation for the move. "They say the move to an empty downtown office building is to illustrate Miami architect Andrés Duany's belief that having people live in the downtown area will help revitalize it," Swartz wrote of the couple the newspaper had dubbed "Stuart's first family."

Among the items sold at auction were a Hawaiian marionette in a grass skirt, a ceramic pie holder in the shape of a cherry pie, a theater-style popcorn popper, four 1948 issues of the *Saturday Evening Post* and the aforementioned Mexican skeleton candelabra.

In their new adventure, the Jeffersons would pool their resources with David and Ann MacMillan, who, at least at the start, weren't really friends of theirs. According to Joan Jefferson, it was more of a partnership of convenience. The MacMillans had some money and know-how needed for the arcade's extreme makeover.

"We were acquaintances," Jefferson said of the MacMillans decades later. "And they had already done some historic preservation building. And they seemed like a natural."

Ann MacMillan remembered the couples first met years earlier while she and David were on a leisurely drive through Palm City. The Jeffersons were working on Common Place, a commercial development Peter Jefferson was designing. "We drove down the road and there's this little house and a lady on top of it painting the roof," Ann MacMillan remembered. "And we stopped and said 'hi' and that was Joan."

That began a relationship that lasted decades, up to and through the point during the 1980s when things were starting to happen downtown.

Post Office Arcade north entrance, 1934. *Martin County Historical Society.*

"We just kind of hooked up with them from the get-go," Ann MacMillan said. "They were a great couple because he [Peter] designed and he had the ideas, and Joanie carried them out and worked right beside him. They were doers. They just saw something and they did it."

In 1990, the Jeffersons and MacMillans closed on the purchase of the Post Office Arcade for $475,000.

Joan Jefferson said the challenges involved in the restoration project were obvious from the outset. "The place was a mess," she said in an interview decades later. "There were rats running around the building." The rodents apparently weren't a strong enough deterrent to discourage the building's new inhabitants.

At the same time the Jeffersons and MacMillans were working together to restore the building, the Jeffersons were actually living and working there. The decision to move into the building was important, from a symbolic and practical standpoint, because one of the ideas Andrés Duany had encouraged was increasing the number of live/work spaces downtown, with offices or shops connected to residential apartments or condominiums. Downtown didn't have a lot of examples of those types of buildings, so the Jeffersons were setting an example for how the concept could work.

It would be wonderful to report the couples had the enthusiastic support of their friends and neighbors, but that's not the way it went. At least not in the beginning. "Everyone questioned it," Joan Jefferson said. "We didn't really respond [to skeptics], but we kept doing it. We actually got on our hands and knees and painted the arcade floor, scraped all the paint off of windows that had been covered over."

The changes were more than superficial. "Peter cut a hole in the roof and created a courtyard," Joan Jefferson said. "The house was built around the courtyard. My office and his office were in the front, then the house wrapped around."

That alteration notwithstanding, Ann MacMillan said one of the goals was to preserve the building's historic feel, particularly on the exterior. "We tried to keep it as original as we could," MacMillan said. "We had people sitting on the streets waiting for us to finish so they could come in and rent."

The skeptics started to take notice as the renovation work progressed. "We laughed at it until the Jeffersons started to make changes," said Nancy Smith, the former *Stuart News* editor. "Then we could see what they saw. You could see the possibilities because they did—and they explained them."

"It was so cool," Richard Geisinger, the Lyric board member, said of the restored arcade building. "It had this inside courtyard. I'll never forget it. I get chills down my back just thinking about it.

"Imagine picking up and moving to this place in a desolate downtown. But Peter did just a great job renovating it that it was a cool place to be."

Peter Jefferson's design expertise was certainly key to the project, but the two wives provided much of the sweat equity. "Peter was an architect and David was a surgeon, so it fell on Ann and I to do it," Joan Jefferson said.

The renovation included sprucing up the building's trademark arch entryway, as well as adding more bathrooms, a new air conditioning system and improvements to the roof.

Joan Jefferson said years later she couldn't remember how much the renovations cost, other than "a lot."

In an August 1, 1991 article in the *Martin County News*, Joan Jefferson said the goal was to create a space where businesses could thrive in a more traditional setting than what the new malls were offering. "Malls are so predictable—people are tired to death of it," she told the newspaper. "We think people want uniqueness and judging from our success, this is true."

Indeed, people were seeing progress each day. And they were seeing the Jeffersons "commuting" to work with only a few steps.

Joan Jefferson said the time she and Peter lived in the arcade was the best part of their marriage. The couple loved being in the heart of downtown, close to shopping and restaurants and recreational amenities. "We sold one of our cars because we didn't need two cars," Joan said. "We could walk to everything."

The Jeffersons were social butterflies who loved showing off their home to visitors. Nancy Smith said the couple would throw lavish parties that took weeks to plan. "You really didn't feel like you were anybody until you got invited to Joan's parties," Smith said. "She was not a diva. She just helped out with everything."

In addition to the Jeffersons' architectural firm, Ann MacMillan was operating a bookstore in one of the building's retail spaces.

Ann MacMillan also remembers that period of time fondly. "We all grew up together," she said. "It was a lot of fun and a lot of work."

It wasn't long before other business owners took note of what was happening at the arcade and wanted to be part of it. "Before you knew it, there was an art gallery setting up there," Smith said. "All of the sudden, some restaurants came in and you just felt like, 'this is it.' People were believers."

In addition to cafés, other early tenants included a convenience store for European goods and an export shop specializing in South American goods.

Aerial photograph, downtown Stuart, circa 1948. *Martin County Library System.*

Joan Jefferson said the entire building was leased within a year "and it was never empty again."

Beyond the value of putting one historic building back to use, the renovation of the Post Office Arcade had a lasting impact on Stuart's collective civic psyche.

Jeff Krauskopf, the former city commissioner, recalled a conversation he and his business partner, Ralph Parks, had with Joan Jefferson before the renovation plans were made public. Jefferson asked Krauskopf and Parks to meet with her at the building. "She said, 'What would you think if we decided to buy this?' Ralph and I looked at each other and he said, 'Why?'" Krauskopf recalled.

Jefferson kept pressing the two men for details about what they thought was a hypothetical renovation project. "We were starting to wrap it [the conversation] up and she said, 'Come over here and I'll show you where our bedroom is.' And I went, 'Huh?'" Krauskopf said. "And she said, 'We bought it.'"

It was at that moment that Krauskopf said he realized how committed the Jeffersons were to reviving downtown.

"She said, 'Jeff, I'm tired of listening to this [complaints about downtown]. We need to pick up the football and carry it down the field ourselves,'" Krauskopf said. "That instant, that singular instant, was when she got the cataracts off of my eyes and I could see clearly. She was willing to put her own money where her mouth was."

The Jeffersons did get a return on their investment. When the two couples sold the building post-restoration, they got $1 million, more than double what they had paid for it. From there, the Jeffersons moved to a property they had been using as a summer home in Highlands, North Carolina.

The couple had a rule in their relationship: in alternating decades, one spouse's priorities would take precedence over the other's. In the 1990s, after a decade of pursuing Joan's dreams to restore downtown Stuart to glory, it was Peter's turn. As Joan explained years later, "Peter wanted to do mountain architecture."

Years later, they returned to Florida when Joan Jefferson got a job directing Florida's Main Street program. Following that, Joan returned to Stuart, where she has lived since Peter's passing.

Before they left for North Carolina, though, the Jeffersons helped set in motion positive momentum that changed downtown's trajectory for the better. Krauskopf described the arcade restoration project as "the spark" and "the lightning bolt" that ignited a fire that couldn't be squelched.

Chapter 19

"MOVING UP SYNDROME" BRINGS NEW RESIDENTS TO STUART

D owntown's revitalization was still a work in progress as the 1980s drew to a close. Many parts of Andrés Duany's master plan had been implemented, but others had not. The discussions about the new Roosevelt Bridge and the long-discussed downtown marina were still ongoing.

Yet as the new decade began, people were starting to take notice that Stuart was a changed place. Stuart won the Governor's 1990 Urban Design Award for commercial revitalization.

The *Stuart News* offered a progress report of sorts in an editorial published on August 10, 1990. The newspaper acknowledged the renovation work had its share of critics. "Somebody thinks the older buildings are ugly; another doesn't like the color of the new sidewalks; someone else thinks the new bandstand is too big; other people moan about parking. And so it goes."

Those complaints considered, the *News* suggested that it was hard to argue progress wasn't being made. "Think back just one decade," the editorial said. "In 1980 there was genuine fear that the city's original commercial district was in an irreversible decline. Structures were falling into disrepair, some stores stood empty, and business stagnated. Back then, not many people complained about a parking shortage downtown, because too few people bothered to go downtown."

Around the mid-1980s, the newspaper noted how community leaders realized downtown's decline needed to be reversed. They oversaw repairs and replacement for underground drainage and sewer lines. They repaved and landscaped the streets. They converted the old courthouse into a cultural arts center and built a riverwalk promenade along the St. Lucie River. "Although much remains to be done, at least there is renewed interest in downtown Stuart," the editorial said. "Even the complaints about insufficient parking can be taken as an indirect compliment. It means more people want to go downtown for business, shopping, dining and entertainment."

The editorial pointed out revitalization might never completely cease but would remain an ongoing goal to pursue. "To our eyes, downtown Stuart looks better now than it has in many years."

It wasn't just Stuart's hometown newspaper that was taking notice. Florida has a long history of attracting migrants from northern states. However, in some cases, people who moved to the Miami and Fort Lauderdale metro areas were realizing those communities were too crowded, too expensive, too crime ridden or combinations of all three. Many of the disillusioned newcomers were moving north to Stuart to take advantage of a slower-paced but more desirable lifestyle.

One magazine described this northward migration from other South Florida communities as "moving up syndrome." In a lengthy cover story published on August 12, 1990, *Sunshine* magazine hailed Stuart as "South Florida's new frontier."

"This former railroad town has grown into a seaside paradise with all the charms of Old Florida," the article said. "But will it become another Fort Lauderdale?"

Children dressed as sprites on Flagler Avenue, January 28, 1926. *Martin County Library System.*

The article contained interviews with several people who had moved to Stuart after initially settling in communities farther south. "The migration began in the '60s but has become a steady flow in recent years as residents of Broward, Palm Beach and Dade go in search of that elusive paradise known as Old Florida," the article said.

The magazine hailed Stuart's four-story limit on building heights as one example of the steps local leaders had taken to make living there a less crowded and more pleasing experience. Looking at the coastal skyline from offshore, the magazine writer noted it was easy to distinguish Martin County from St. Lucie County to the north and Palm Beach County to the south.

With the height restrictions, Martin County looked like "a missing tooth" in a jaw full of teeth made up of high-rise condominiums. "While Vero Beach also is known for its resistance to high-density development, no city outclasses Stuart when it comes to environmental awareness," the magazine article said.

Sunshine described Stuart as an upscale community, with prominent families like the Kiplingers and the Evinrudes taking up residence there. The Kiplingers ran a business media publishing empire, and the Evinrudes were titans in the boating industry.

"Despite its yuppie image, Stuart doesn't really have a drawbridge mentality," the article said. "But it is proud of its castle and is not ready to be overrun by urban barbarians."

The article also made a bold prediction about Stuart that didn't quite come true. "Because it is the county seat of a rapidly growing area, Stuart is no longer a sleepy little town near the ocean," the article said. "But because it has nothing resembling the concrete canyons of Dade and Broward, most people don't realize that it is destined to become a major South Florida metropolis during the next two decades."

While Stuart grew quite a bit, it hadn't reached metropolis status as the twenty-first century began. The U.S. Census Bureau considers Stuart, and all of Martin and St. Lucie Counties, to be part of Port St. Lucie's metro area.

The magazine article, while predicting a growth surge, also suggested it might be a blessing in disguise that many of the newcomers were arriving from counties to the south. "It's probably a good thing so many people come here from Fort Lauderdale and Miami because of what has happened there," Kip Myers, an advertising executive, said in an interview with the magazine. "They have seen all the mistakes you can make with growth, and they're determined not to make those mistakes again."

The region's larger newspapers like the *Palm Beach Post* and *Miami Herald* were also writing articles describing Stuart as a great place to visit or live. "From blighted, boarded-up, semi-deserted streets, the downtown became one of the most promising retail areas around," the *Palm Beach Post* said in a January 27, 1991 article. "Some local shopping centers are having trouble keeping stores, but downtown Stuart has attracted dozens of businesses."

A September 29, 1991 article in the *Miami Herald* took particular note of downtown Stuart's many "retro" design touches. "Somehow, today's cars just don't fit in along the streets of downtown Stuart," the article began. "Model Ts would be more appropriate, with an occasional Packard or Duesenberg. They would add the finishing touch to a downtown recently restored to look as it did 60 or 70 years ago."

The *Herald* writer liked the Mediterranean Revival buildings with stucco façades, old-fashioned streetlights, wooden park benches and a certain bronze statue from 1938. (Remember her?)

The antique touches were also on display inside many downtown buildings. Some shops had wood moldings, hardwood floors and antique furniture. The article noted the mosaic tile floor in the Ashley restaurant, formerly the Bank of Stuart, dated to 1912.

Other buildings cited as harkening back to earlier times included the old Art Deco courthouse, the "quaint" red clapboard Stuart Feed Store and the "Mediterranean-style" Post Office Arcade, as well as a number of well-preserved Cracker houses.

"Downtown Stuart will never offer the malls' convenience of having everything under one roof," the *Herald* article said. "But neither will the malls offer a restored 1912 bank that stocks a first edition of 'Life on the Mississippi.'"

The *Herald* had more to say about downtown Stuart a couple of years later. "Stuart's charming old downtown area grew shabby as merchants moved away and vagrants moved into echoing storefronts," an August 7, 1994 *Herald* article said. "Finally, local loyalists dug in and began breathing new zing into Art Deco architectural treasures. Today in its revitalized downtown, Stuart's old town square is the focal point of a smart streetscape of parks, historic buildings, restaurants, galleries, and shops, all of them still far enough removed from U.S. 1 that they are bypassed by everyday traffic."

Joan Jefferson, who had served as a city commissioner and mayor while the revitalization work was ongoing, drew her share of media acclaim. She also took some criticism from people who said, as a resident and owner

Flagler Avenue, circa 1945. *Martin County Library System.*

of the Post Office Arcade, she was personally profiting from some of the projects that were initiated during her time as a city official.

City Manager Jack Noble addressed those allegations in a January 13, 1992 *Stuart News* article. "No one else was willing to go down there and do what she did," Noble said. "The bummest rap she is getting is somehow she foresaw all this happening. Downtown is still in a developing stage, and there are still no guarantees."

Jefferson's admirers outnumbered her detractors, though. During the 1990s, she was invited to make a presentation at the Second Congress for the New Urbanism.

A January 12, 1992 *Stuart News* editorial lamented the end of what it called the "Jeffersonian Era in Stuart." The editorial noted that Jefferson, the first woman to serve as the city's mayor, had been "a lightning rod for criticism—sometimes bitter, and frequently undeserved."

The editorial dismissed the conflict-of-interests allegations that had been leveled against Jefferson since she and her husband had undertaken the Post Office Arcade restoration. "It's an odd accusation, considering that many key decisions about downtown already had been made by then," the editorial said. "Also, the Jeffersons were willing to gamble their own money to show faith in a downtown revival at a time when investing there was a very risky business."

In summing up Jefferson's contributions to the city, the editorial suggested Stuart would have looked much different if she hadn't come onto the scene. "It's difficult to say what Stuart would be like today without the Joan Jefferson influence," the editorial said. "We have a strong hunch that, had it not been for her ability to draw people together to work for common goals, many good things done in the past decade would never have been accomplished."

A September 2, 1994 *Stuart News* article chronicled the Jeffersons' plans to relocate to Highlands, North Carolina, at least temporarily. The article said Joan Jefferson would continue to serve as the Post Office Arcade's manager remotely. Ann MacMillan planned to expand her store, the Arcade Book Nook, into the Jeffersons' old living space in the building after the couple departed.

Joan Jefferson was talking about writing a book, explaining the concepts of New Urbanism in plain language. "We proved the point" that New Urbanism could work, Jefferson told the *News*.

Palm Beach Post columnist Nisha Pulliam wrote a lighthearted column about Jefferson's farewell party for the newspaper's February 12, 1992 edition. Invitations dubbed the event a "Go to Hell party." Jefferson was jokingly coronated "Queen of Downtown." The festivities included a tongue-in-cheek listing of other jobs Jefferson could take, including rewrite editor for *Palm Beach Post* journalists Sally Swartz and Scott Shifrel and lead actress in the Barn Theater's production of *Some Like It Hot*.

In keeping with the party's lighthearted theme, Jeff Krauskopf, Jefferson's colleague on the city commission, showed up with a "Jefferson for County Commission" campaign sign. Jefferson was photographed for Pulliam's column wearing a sailboat hat, complete with a miniature bag of garbage, at the event.

One other footnote from the 1990s: in 1991, the Lady Abundance statue, which a *Stuart News* editorial dubbed as "downtown's darling," was moved from Memorial Park to its current home in Haney Circle.

Joan Jefferson and Lady Abundance both became powerful symbols of Stuart's resilience and prosperity. In time, they both got their due recognition.

Chapter 20

WHAT MAKES DOWNTOWN STUART "WORK"?

A s one of those *Miami Herald* articles referenced in the last chapter said, downtown Stuart can't compare with the "everything under one roof" convenience of shopping malls, which were nearing the height of their popularity during the 1980s. However, the central business district has so many other advantages going for it that it has continued to thrive over the last three decades even as malls and other large shopping centers have become less attractive options for visitors.

One obvious reason is downtown Stuart is much more than just a place to shop. There are parks where kids can play and adults can catch their breath. One of the most popular is the park adjacent to the courthouse, with a gazebo that provides a shady refuge during the heat of the Florida summer. There's a large grassy area that hosts farmers' markets on weekends. The open space provided there and at other spots downtown creates a less congested atmosphere.

There's a riverwalk that offers stunning views of the St. Lucie River. The river still faces challenges with pollution, much of it originating from Lake Okeechobee and points north, but city leaders have done what they could to prevent sewage discharges into the river. The city continues to lobby the U.S. Army Corps of Engineers and state and federal environmental agencies in support of other efforts to reduce the number of water discharges from Lake Okeechobee and has adopted other measures, including an ordinance that regulates fertilizer use, in an attempt to reduce pollutants.

There are park benches where people can rest, giving Stuart a much more laid-back vibe than the downtowns in many larger cities that seem to thrive on hustle and bustle.

There are lots of other elements that go into creating that vibe, too. Many of the buildings downtown have beautiful architecture, like the Art Deco old courthouse, the Mediterranean-style Post Office Arcade and the Lyric Theatre. The streets are decorated with vintage lampposts, flower-filled planters and sidewalks decorated with embedded paver stones. There are generous amounts of public art sprinkled throughout downtown, some sculptures or statues like Lady Abundance, plus murals, mosaics and other decorative touches.

While locals occasionally grumble about the parking situation, there are actually many spaces available within a reasonable walking distance from the shops and restaurants clustered on or near Flagler and Osceola.

There's still some grumbling about Confusion Corner, although it seems residents would rather have it remain a roundabout with a baffling number of roads feeding into it, as opposed to a standard intersection with traffic lights or stop signs. Confusion Corner could have been "fixed" a long time ago, if the political will were there. However, as the Department of Transportation discovered during the years it was planning for the new Roosevelt Bridge, some locals are willing to fight to preserve the status quo.

Confusion Corner is a landmark that makes Stuart different from other cities. Being able to negotiate it without having a nervous breakdown is a trait longtime residents embrace as a badge of honor. Thomas Weber, the former *Stuart News* editor, may have been right when he suggested Confusion Corner is sort of like an initiation test. If newcomers can't manage to play nice with other motorists at Confusion Corner, they might have the wrong kind of temperament to handle Stuart's good-natured lifestyle.

These are just a few examples of the factors that make visiting downtown Stuart a pleasant experience, as opposed to just a place to buy goods or services. You can have fun in downtown Stuart without spending a lot of money.

Downtown Stuart has been fortunate in its ability to attract a lot of quality restaurants and shops. Many of those shops are geared more to luxury and comfort items than providing essentials. If people are looking for plumbing supplies or flooring tiles, there are probably places in outlying neighborhoods better equipped to handle those types of purchases. However, for those who want a piece of artwork or some other uniquely Florida gift to send to folks living up north, downtown Stuart is a great place to look.

The dining options range from casual pizza joints to high-end steakhouses. There are multiple places to grab a cup of coffee or an ice cream cone downtown.

Downtown is much more than just a place to shop. In addition to the afore-mentioned parks, there are other entertainment amenities, like the riverwalk amphitheater. Bands play there on a regular basis. And the Lyric is more than a pretty building to admire. It's not a large enough venue to host a Taylor Swift concert or other large events, but it's an intimate setting for comedy shows, musicals and other performances that don't require a ton of seating. The theater's retro styling adds to the charm of any event held there.

Women's Club of Stuart, circa 1965. *Martin County Library System.*

The Stuart Feed Store houses an excellent museum on local history. It's a great place to spend a few minutes, or longer, out of the Florida sun.

There are trams that provide not only transportation but also tour guides who offer primers on local points of interest. Walking and bicycling also feel like safe and viable options, which is not the case in many larger cities.

Downtown Stuart also features many beautiful homes, some in the Old Florida bungalow style found farther south in Key West, within easy walking distance of downtown's core. Throughout downtown, the buildings seem well matched to each other in terms of scale and character, thanks to rules like the four-story height restriction.

Importantly, downtown Stuart feels safe, without the crime that discourages people from visiting some larger cities.

Comparing downtown Stuart to a conventional shopping center, enclosed or otherwise, really misses the point. People visit downtown Stuart for the same reasons they visit places like St. Augustine; Charleston, South Carolina; Williamsburg, Virginia; or even a few larger cities like San Francisco and New Orleans.

It's an overall experience visitors want to have.

Downtown Stuart delivers that in spades.

Chapter 21

FOLLOWING STUART'S RECIPE FOR SUCCESS

The revitalization of Stuart's downtown during the 1980s and 1990s is, in some ways, a "bad news, good news" story.

The bad news is, the urban blight and deterioration that happened in Stuart can and has happened in a lot of other places, too. It's fairly easy to understand why. Any city's downtown is more than likely one of its oldest neighborhoods. In many cases, downtown is the first part of a city that's settled and developed, with growth sprouting from it in a series of suburban rings. So downtown is often a city's first neighborhood. That means older buildings. Older streets. Older water and sewer lines. Older buildings and infrastructure fall into disrepair unless they're properly maintained.

Older neighborhoods sometimes lose their coolness, too. As new neighborhoods are built around them, some homebuyers and business owners will inevitably be attracted to their newness. When buying cars, the new models on the showroom floor tend to sell the best. Used cars are perceived as less desirable, which means their value declines year after year. There are a few exceptions to this—the 1965 Ford Mustangs or 1957 Chevrolet Bel Airs of the world—but a similar principle is often at work as people evaluate the value of different neighborhoods within a city. Does a neighborhood have "curb appeal," with freshly paved streets and modern-looking houses with gleaming new coats of paint? If a downtown has been neglected, its curb appeal may be lacking.

Did "big box" chain retailers put the mom-and-pop shops that used to populate downtown out of business? Did some of the professional services firms downtown move to office parks where they could build to their own specifications and have room to expand? Did residents ditch downtown apartments and condominiums in favor of new subdivisions with houses no one else had lived in yet?

It happens. If it hasn't happened in a particular city yet, it probably will in due time.

So that's the bad news.

The good news is that many of the steps Stuart took to revitalize its downtown can be replicated in other communities. All communities are different, of course, and not everything that worked in Stuart will work somewhere else. Conversely, some of the things that didn't work in Stuart might be just what another community needs to succeed.

In Stuart's case, having some dynamic community leaders come along at the right time in the city's history certainly helped. Joan and Peter Jefferson are widely credited with not only launching initiatives that helped save downtown but also inspiring others to consider how they might get involved.

"We laughed at it [downtown] until the Jeffersons started making changes," said former *Stuart News* editor Nancy Smith. "Then we could see what they saw. We saw what it could be. We saw the possibilities."

"I think you have to give Joan and Peter credit for this whole thing," said Thomas Weber, another former Stuart News editor. "They developed a viable plan for saving the architecture of old Stuart."

Richard Geisinger, the former Lyric Theatre board member, said the couple had skills that complemented each other well. "It was [Joan's] stamina, her vision, and Peter's creative side," Geisinger said.

Jeff Krauskopf, the former city commissioner, said his former colleague was able to energize residents toward a common purpose. "She whipped us into shape," he said of Joan Jefferson. "When you felt her commitment, her willingness to roll up her sleeves, you wanted to be a part of that."

Andrés Duany's involvement was certainly one of the keys to downtown Stuart's rebirth. Duany has established himself as one of the biggest names, if not the biggest name, in urban planning over the last four decades or so. However, he got involved with the Stuart downtown plan fairly early in his career. He was known within the urban planning industry at the time, primarily for his work on Seaside, but his accolades—and the demand for his services—have only increased through the years. (As this book is being written, he's involved in assisting Vero Beach, a community about an hour's drive north of Stuart, in developing a plan for its downtown.)

Of course, having Duany's recommendations wouldn't have meant much unless the community's leaders and its residents were open-minded enough to consider implementing them. Krauskopf said it might be difficult for another city to muster the kind of unity that was present in Stuart during those days. "I can't stress enough how the press and the community got behind it all," Krauskopf said. "At the time, there was trust and respect among the commissioners and the staff."

Krauskopf said we're living in a different era now, when political divisiveness is more prevalent and difficult to overcome. "Things were much different then," he said. "People could disagree, but we civilly listened to each other, thought about it, and everyone was willing to entertain everyone else's views."

Krauskopf said the business community mobilized behind the renovation plans because shop owners could see no better alternatives.

Ann MacMillan, the Jeffersons' partner in the Post Office Arcade project, said the business community's support was born in large part out of frustration over the neighborhood's economic decline. "Part of it is getting angry," MacMillan said. "You have to get pissed and angry and want to make a change."

Downtown paving work, April 1990. *Sandra Thurlow photo collection.*

Taking small steps, like that community service day held in the early 1980s, emboldened residents to take on bigger and even more impactful initiatives in the years that followed.

On the technical side of things, Joan Jefferson said adopting an architectural code for the city was a critical ingredient in maintaining downtown's character through the years.

Looking back on what his predecessors did, former city commissioner Troy McDonald said the formation of the Main Street organization was an important factor. The Main Street program, administered through the state, provides ideas and technical assistance to cities large and small. It's also helpful to have an organization closely allied with city government that has protecting and improving downtown as its first and last priority.

McDonald said developing a unified vision for downtown was another important step. That can be more easily said than done, given most communities have many stakeholders with sometimes competing interests.

Another subtle but important step, in McDonald's eyes, was setting limits on the number and size of establishments selling alcoholic beverages within the neighborhood. Downtown Stuart has its share of bars and restaurants, but the limits ensure there's room for other businesses, too, so the neighborhood isn't just a nighttime and weekend party spot.

Part of Stuart's success is owed to having such a good mix of businesses with unique character. Downtown isn't filled with chain stores or restaurants that can be found throughout the country. Mom-and-pop businesses have managed to survive and even thrive there.

Chapter 22

JOAN JEFFERSON GETS HER WAY

t's one thing to be the city's first female mayor, who many say was the spark that led to downtown revitalization," Suzanne Wentley's article in the August 26, 2001 edition of the *Stuart News* began. "It's another thing altogether to have a street named after you."

The Stuart City Commission had decided the week before to rename Second Street as Joan Jefferson Way. The idea grew out of a discussion about installing a roundabout at Second Street and Dixie Highway. As a companion to that project, the Stuart Main Street group suggested renaming Second as, well, "Main Street."

Then–city manager David Collier had a different idea. "It's time the people who originated the push that resulted in the success of historic downtown be recognized," he told the newspaper reporter. "I was surprised how quickly [commissioners] said, 'Yeah, let's do it.'"

Among the commissioners voting for the change was Commissioner Charles Foster, who had frequently been at odds with Jefferson during the years he and Joan served on the commission together.

Wentley's article noted Jefferson had served on the commission from 1979 to 1983 and then again from 1987 to 1992. "When Jefferson began her stint as a commissioner, downtown was filled with 'for rent' signs, peeling paint and struggling stores," Wentley wrote.

The article noted Jefferson's role in organizing a $1 million renovation project along Osceola Street and Flagler Avenue during the late 1980s. And, of course, the article referenced the Jeffersons' partnership with the

MacMillans to restore the Post Office Arcade. "They [the Jeffersons] bought that run-down, beat-up building and improved it," said James Christie, who also served on the commission with Joan Jefferson. "They were the catalyst for the type of renaissance for what happened."

Wentley noted the changes initiated during the 1980s and 1990s had held up well through the years that had passed. "Now, with barely any vacancies in the historic downtown and rents rising steadily, few say the renovation plans weren't a success," she wrote.

Jefferson, by that point living with Peter in their Highland, North Carolina home, said she was "very humbled" by the street renaming and noted many people were involved in downtown's resurgence. "We hoped it wouldn't be a three-street wonder and that it would permeate throughout the city of Stuart and everyone would benefit from what we started here," Jefferson said. "The citizens and the staff who came after us deserve credit, too."

At this writing, more than two decades after the street renaming, Joan Jefferson Way signs still greet visitors entering downtown from the north on the new Roosevelt Bridge. The stoplight at US 1 and Joan Jefferson Way marks one of the entrances to the historic downtown area.

During her years as a commissioner, Jefferson fought for the bridge realignment that saved many of the historic buildings from being plowed under in the name of progress. Now her name sits on a sign at the bridge's southern end, as if Jefferson's spirit is on sentry duty, guarding her prized work from those who would do it harm.

Thousands of motorists pass through the intersection of US 1 and Joan Jefferson Way each day. During the morning and evening rush hours, cars sit at red lights, staring up at that sign. Many are tourists or newcomers who more than likely have no idea who Joan Jefferson was or what her contributions to the city were. The old-timers know, though. Although many are getting up in their years, they haven't forgotten.

There was a time when downtown Stuart seemed destined for ruin and decay. Then along came Jefferson and a group of other dedicated citizens who were willing to sacrifice their time, energy and money to make sure that didn't happen.

Maybe they'll even get a statue of their own someday.

ABOUT THE AUTHOR

B lake Fontenay is a columnist and editorial writer. He has spent more than twenty-five years as a reporter, columnist and editorial writer for metropolitan daily newspapers, including the *Sacramento Bee*, (Jacksonville) *Florida Times-Union*, *Orlando Sentinel* and (Memphis) *Commercial Appeal*. He has won numerous awards for column and editorial writing in Tennessee, Colorado and Florida.

During an eight-year break from the newspaper business, he worked as the communications director for Tennessee's comptroller, treasurer and secretary of state.

His debut novel, *The Politics of Barbecue*, was published by John F. Blair Publisher in September 2012. *The Politics of Barbecue* won the Independent Publishers Book Awards gold medal for fiction in the South region in 2013.

Other published works include the novels *Scouts' Honor* and *A Three Team Town*.